# THE HIDDEN
## STORY OF JACOB

### What we can see in Hebrew
### that we cannot see in English

Eli Lizorkin-Eyzenberg, Ph.D.

ISBN: 9781797554167

# DEDICATION

To my beautiful boys
Tomer, Vlad, Oren and Moshe.

May you never forget
the road Jacob traveled.

# Contents

# CHAPTER ONE: THE HIDDEN STORY OF JACOB

Jacob is one of the most fascinating characters in the entire Hebrew Bible. His story and the story of his children are some of the greatest stories ever told. Some details of his life remain hidden to most people because they cannot read the original Hebrew. Translations often fail to convey everything the Hebrew text reveals. I hope to help you see some of the details hidden and obscured by English translations. So, let us begin in the beginning.

## The Struggle in the Womb

The story of Jacob begins with his mother Rebekah's initial inability to conceive. Rebekah's barrenness confirms upon her a line of succession to her late mother-in-law – Sarah (Gen. 24.67). Although the story of Rebekah is much more compressed and less complex than the corresponding story of Sarah (Gen. 16), the parallel is obvious and intentional. As her pregnancy advanced, Rebekah felt vigorous movements of what turned out to be two children in her womb (Esau and Jacob). She inquired of the LORD about the intense struggle that she felt going on inside her.

The babies' movements in her womb were but a sign, foretelling the relationship they would have as siblings. It indicated their separate, but related, purposes in God's plan. The Hebrew word for "struggle" used in the text speaks of a struggle that is very intense, harsh, even conveying the sense of a crushing battle. When Rebekah petitioned the Lord about her situation, He answered her:

וַיֹּאמֶר יהוה לָהּ שְׁנֵי גֹיִים בְּבִטְנֵךְ וּשְׁנֵי לְאֻמִּים מִמֵּעַיִךְ יִפָּרֵדוּ וּלְאֹם מִלְאֹם יֶאֱמָץ
וְרַב יַעֲבֹד צָעִיר:

*"Two nations are in your womb, two separate peoples shall issue from your body; One people shall be mightier than the other, and the older shall serve the younger."* *(Gen. 25:23)*

We can appreciate how the translators saw what we also see, i.e. the literal and unambiguous meaning, but struggled with how to best translate the intricacies of Hebrew for the greatest benefit of their readers. They sought to keep two very important factors in balance: the accuracy of the text translated, and its readability. To find an equivalent to Hebrew in another language is not always easy and sometimes not possible. Therefore, the translators used the *dynamic equivalence method* – that is, instead of translating *word-for-word*, they translated *thought-for-thought*. Some English language translations adopt this method even when it is possible to translate word-for-word, preferring the increased readability (with essential meaning preserved) to a more literal translation (with original wording preserved).

Often it is very helpful to see a literal translation in order to appreciate that the vast majority of Bible translations, such as the one above (NJPS), use *dynamic equivalence* rather than a strictly *literal* method of translation. It is important to keep in mind that a more literal translation is not necessarily more faithful. Meaning can be diluted and easily lost by preserving obscure grammatical structures of another language. Nevertheless, reading a text translated from Hebrew literally can enrich our understanding of the text (especially if we know some Hebrew). This practice always safeguards us from thinking that translations are free from interpretive errors and can be trusted uncritically.

When translated literally we see this idea: "Two peoples are in your stomach" שְׁנֵי גֹיִים בְּבִטְנֵךְ *(shene goyim be-vitnekh)*. "And two peoples from your body will be separated [from each other]" וּשְׁנֵי לְאֻמִּים מִמֵּעַיִךְ יִפָּרֵדוּ *(u-shene leumim mi-meayikh yiparedu)*. "One people from another people will exercise effort/strength" וּלְאֹם מִלְאֹם יֶאֱמָץ *(u-leom mi-leom yeemats)*. It is the last portion of this verse that introduces a considerable ambiguity וְרַב יַעֲבֹד צָעִיר *(ve-rav yaavod tsair)*. Traditional translations render it as "the older will serve the younger." However, there is a potential problem with such translation. The Hebrew phrase is indefinite; it does not say "the older" or "the younger" but literally just "great" and "young." If the words were definite, it would include the particle אֵת *(et)* to indicate the direct object. Without that marker, the text is not entirely clear as to whether the younger will serve the older or the other way around, since Hebrew syntax can sometimes be flexible.

The second feature alerting us to an ambiguity is that we expect the opposite of "young" צָעִיר *(tsair)* to be "old," not רַב *(rav)* "great/big" as is written here in Hebrew. English translations set the sentence up as if the two opposites are in view (younger vs. older). Can you imagine having to make a translation decision when the text in Hebrew clearly has a built-in ambiguity? The text of Genesis then goes on to tell the reader that when Rebekah did give birth, it became clear that she was not imagining things – the twins, still struggling with each other, were finally born (Gen. 25:24-26). We read the detailed description of this birth as follows:

וַיֵּצֵא הָרִאשׁוֹן אַדְמוֹנִי כֻּלּוֹ כְּאַדֶּרֶת שֵׂעָר וַיִּקְרְאוּ שְׁמוֹ עֵשָׂו:

*The first one emerged red, like a hairy mantle all over; so they named him Esau. (Gen. 25:25)*

When Esau, the first of the twins, emerged his appearance determined both his name and the name of the nations that would proceed from him. The word אַדְמוֹנִי *(admoni)* is related to the word for "Adam" אָדָם *(adam)* and other words, such as אָדֹם *(adom)* "red" and אֲדָמָה *(adamah)* "earth." We should also not forget the sound similarity with דָּם *(dam)* "blood." This is why the people group descended from Esau was called Edom or the Edomites. Esau became the father of the Edomites, and Jacob the father of the Israelites. These two nations continued their struggle throughout most of their history. But this baby also needed a name that was

3

somehow connected to him. Those who were present at his birth saw that he was "fully covered with hair" כֻּלּוֹ כְּאַדֶּרֶת שֵׂעָר (kulo ke-aderet sear). Although the etymology of the name "Esau" is unknown, it seems to have something to do with his hairy body. The Hebrew word for "hair" is שֵׂעָר (sear) and for "Esau" עֵשָׂו (Esav).

The connection between these words is unclear. Nonetheless, there are cases in which words do have root connections in Biblical Hebrew even if this is not obvious at first glance. Possibly there was once a root word that meant "hair" which fell out of use in Hebrew (עָשָׂה). The Biblical Hebrew root word from those letters עָשָׂה (asah) means "to make" or "to do." This Semitic root does also survive, interestingly enough, in the Arabic language (a language related to Hebrew) where it means "hair" or "hairy." Given that there does not seem to be any obvious connection between Esau's birth and "to do/make," the suggestion that this ancient Hebrew root fell out of use is a plausible one. However, this is only one interpretive option. A second one, at least, can be thought of in terms of connection with the above-mentioned Hebrew root עָשָׂה (asah), which carries the meaning of "making and doing." In this scenario the name of Esau has a meaning close to the English expression "fully made" and communicates the idea of being perfect and ready.

On the surface this connection does not seem to work, since we are accustomed to thinking of Esau as a negative character in the story (being very hairy has a negative connotation in the Western world). However, "hairy" does not mean unattractive or have negative connotations in the world of the Bible. If we consider the beginning of the story (Jacob's and Esau's birth) in light of the end of this very story, we see that Esau exhibited a strong, generous, forgiving character. This can be clearly seen in the scene of his reconciliation with Jacob (Gen. 33). None of the stolen blessings were realized during the life of Jacob (especially those having to do with power and domination). In the end, it was Jacob who called Esau "his lord" to his face and prostrated before him seven times, thereby acknowledging his fault in stealing his brother's blessing. Contrary to expectations, Esau is blessed with a good and successful life, free of his brother's unconditional superiority and domination (Gen. 27:39-40).

Jacob does live out the blessing that was intended by Isaac for him from the beginning. It is the second blessing that Isaac gave him which actually comes true in his lifetime. God promised to bless Jacob with the blessing of Abraham and grant him the perpetual inheritance of the Promised Land and offspring (Gen. 28:3-4). While Jacob stole the blessing of wealth and domination, it was the blessing of the land and posterity that God had in mind for him. If we allow ourselves to see Esau in a positive (or at least not exclusively negative) light, then we can see how his name could be related to perfection being "fully made or complete."

In their commentaries, the Jewish sages accurately observed that no one honored his father more than Esau in the Bible. The covenant blessing of land and children, however, had to go through Jacob - not because he earned it, but because God decided that it would be so, for reasons known to God alone.

וְאַחֲרֵי־כֵן יָצָא אָחִיו וְיָדוֹ אֹחֶזֶת בַּעֲקֵב

*Then his brother emerged, holding on to the heel of Esau; so they named him Jacob… (Gen. 25:26)*

When Esau first emerged, they observed something amazing. His twin brother was holding on to his heel, as if not willing to let him go and be born first. Jacob's name in Hebrew יַעֲקֹב *(Yaakov)* relates to the word for "heel" עָקֵב *(akev)*. For this reason his parents called him a "heel-grabber." In modern Hebrew, instead of saying that we are "following someone", we literally say "we are going after their heel לַעֲקֹב אַחֲרֵי מִשֶׁהוּ *(laakov acharei mishehu)*. So it's amusing to think that to "follow someone" could be interpreted as "to Jacob someone."

5

## Trouble in the Making

The Book of Genesis (or at the very least its basic narrative structure) was authored to encourage the Israelites who left Egypt and were struggling with their troubles and identity. It was not written "in real time." In other words, the author of Genesis did not claim that it described events as they were happening at that time. Genesis describes how historical events that took place long ago relate to, determine, and inform the current situation on the ground. The stories are told to speak deeply and convincingly to Israelites (the children of Jacob) who at that moment sought to survive as a people, and eventually, as the covenant promise states, come into the Promised Land and establish themselves as a nation.

The stories of families portrayed in the Bible are brutally honest and oftentimes shock the readers with "naked truth," - the kind of narratives that most families would try very hard to keep private. Take parental favoritism, for example. Today it is considered the gravest of parental sins, but in reality such things often happen. Likewise, the biblical reality of sibling rivalry happens far more often than we like to acknowledge. Parents often do connect better with some children than with others, for a variety of reasons. While it can be said that parents love all their children in same way, it can also be established that they often favor one child over another. In fact, the idea of "disliking, hating or favoring someone less" works quite differently in Biblical Hebrew.

This is especially true when the idea is expressed in contrast to "loving someone." The phraseology expresses the idea of intensity of feeling in comparison. In other words, "Jacob I loved... Esau I hated" (Mal. 1:2-3) is rendered quite literally in our modern terms. Translated from ancient Hebrew and interpreted into our modern way of speaking it could arguably mean something more like "Esau I loved, but Jacob I favored with my great covenantal love." The same is the case with Jesus' statement that one must love Him and hate his parents (Luke 14:26). This is an idiomatic Hebraism that makes a comparison and does not actually instruct one to express hatred towards one's parents. That would be absurd, given God's explicit commandment to honor them.

What is clear is that the Book of Genesis is Torah for all of Israel; it is not a manual on parenting and should not be read as such. The loving and favoring of one child over another is stated as a matter of fact and is not in any way criticized or judged. What is evident from this story, as we will shortly see, is that one of the parents makes a right choice and the other makes a wrong choice regarding which child they chose to favor. If we realize that Genesis was written for Israelites who struggled with Edomites (among others), we will clearly and quickly see why the narrative of Esau and Jacob's births and the choices their parents made were very important to know and to internalize for the original readers/hearers of Genesis. Only when we understand how the texts apply to the original audience for which they were intended, can we ever hope to be able to apply them accurately to our modern times and our very different lives. We read about the continued post-womb struggle of Esau and Jacob in Genesis 25:27-28:

וַיִּגְדְּלוּ הַנְּעָרִים וַיְהִי עֵשָׂו אִישׁ יֹדֵעַ צַיִד אִישׁ שָׂדֶה וְיַעֲקֹב אִישׁ תָּם יֹשֵׁב אֹהָלִים:

*When the boys grew up, Esau became a skillful hunter, a man of the outdoors; but Jacob was a mild man who stayed in camp. (Gen. 25:27)*

וַיֶּאֱהַב יִצְחָק אֶת־עֵשָׂו כִּי־צַיִד בְּפִיו וְרִבְקָה אֹהֶבֶת אֶת־יַעֲקֹב:

*Isaac loved Esau because he had a taste for game, but Rebekah loved Jacob (Gen. 25:28).*

Isaac seems blind (for the time being) to the higher purpose that God has for his son Jacob. These purposes would become clear to the readers of the Genesis account only later. Isaac is blinded by his own personal preferences and connects with Esau better than with Jacob. God's own preference for the younger son over the older has already become a familiar pattern from the story of Cain and Abel (Gen. 4.4-5). The same idea is seen in the narrative of Ishmael and Isaac (Gen. 21:12). This same principle will also become a prominent feature in the story of Joseph and his relationship with his older brothers (Gen. 37:3). While the reason for Rebekah's choice is not given, Isaac's wrong choice is clearly explained. We read in the above-cited Genesis 25:28 וַיֶּאֱהַב יִצְחָק אֶת־עֵשָׂו כִּי־צַיִד בְּפִיו (va-yeehav Yitschak et Esav ki tsayid be-fiv). Translated literally, it would say: "And Isaac loved Esau because hunting was in his (Isaac's) mouth." This expression specifies exactly why Isaac loved Esau more than Jacob – his taste for hunted game.

This may be another point of connection between Isaac and Abraham. When Abraham agreed to take Hagar and endeavor to father a son through her, he too was blinded to God's will because of his natural desire for an heir. Esau's descendants eventually dominated the southern lands and made their living by agriculture and trade. One of the ancient trade routes, the King's Highway (Num. 20:17), passed through Edom, and when the Israelites requested permission to use this route on their exodus from Egypt, they were forcefully forbidden to pass. The Book of Deuteronomy, however, clearly states that Edomites should not be hated by Israelites because they are brothers (Deut. 23:7). Moreover, the warning is issued to Israelites by God not to provoke Edomites because God Himself guarantees Esau's inheritance (Deut. 2:4-5). It is interesting that the prophet Amos connects Edom with all the nations of the world that are called by the name of the LORD (Amos 9:12).

## Not-So-Brotherly Love

Isaac favored towards Esau because he had a taste for hunted game; but Jacob was a mild young man who was described as staying in the camp (Gen. 25:28), and he was favored by his mother, Rebekah. God's favoring of a younger son is already familiar from the story of Cain and Abel (Gen. 4:4-5) and, in a different way, with Ishmael and

Isaac (Gen. 21:12). Later, in Genesis 37:3, it will become the prominent feature of the story of Joseph and his brothers.

The line of thought about God favoring the younger brother in the Esau and Jacob story continues with the account of the "sold" and "bought" birthright. Jacob was "stewing a stew" וַיָּזֶד יַעֲקֹב נָזִיד *(va-yazed Yaakoov nazid)* when Esau came in, וְהוּא עָיֵף *(ve-hu ayef)* "and he was famished/exhausted" from his hunting. Esau had spent an entire day seeking wild meat, not livestock bred and grown in Isaac's family flocks. We read in Genesis 25:30-31:

וַיֹּאמֶר עֵשָׂו אֶל־יַעֲקֹב הַלְעִיטֵנִי נָא מִן־הָאָדֹם הָאָדֹם הַזֶּה כִּי עָיֵף אָנֹכִי עַל־כֵּן קָרָא־
שְׁמוֹ אֱדוֹם:

*And Esau said to Jacob, "Give me some of that red stuff to gulp down, for I am famished" – which is why he was named Edom. (Gen. 25:30)*

The Hebrew word Esau used to tell Jacob to "feed him" is הַלְעִיטֵנִי *(haliteni)* which communicates the idea of "devouring greedily/gulping down," or translated even more literally "cause/enable me to devour greedily." The Hebrew phrase that Esau used to describe the "stew" נָזִיד *(nazid)* mentioned earlier is מִן־הָאָדֹם הָאָדֹם *(min ha-adom ha-adom)* or literally "from this red-red (thing)." This event with stew is very significant in the greater story. It is so significant that the later connection of Esau with his posterity, the Edomites, is rooted in this explanation: "which is why he was named Edom" עַל־כֵּן קָרָא־שְׁמוֹ אֱדוֹם *(al ken kara shemo Edom)*. We must understand that "red" and "Edom" are closely related words in Hebrew.

It is intriguing that the word translated as "stew" in the text (vs.29) is נָזִיד *(nazid)*, which means something like "the thing boiled." However, the verb related to this noun, in addition to the meaning "to boil," sometimes can mean "to presume" or even "to act proudly/arrogantly." If this connection is meant to be seen in the story, then perhaps the author seeks to align the reader's sympathies

9

not with Jacob, but with Esau. He is the hardworking family man; the son that his father can be proud of in a good sense. Is Jacob going about his milder affairs with pride or a heart full of presumption? We don't know; but the story will seek at times to evoke sympathy for the one who will not be chosen to continue the covenantal line of blessing. Though not chosen, Esau will be greatly loved and personally protected by Israel's God.

וַיֹּאמֶר יַעֲקֹב מִכְרָה כַיּוֹם אֶת־בְּכֹרָתְךָ לִי:

*Jacob said, "First sell me your birthright." (Gen. 25:31)*

Now Jacob, seeing his older brother's weakness, demands that Esau should מִכְרָה כַיּוֹם אֶת־בְּכֹרָתְךָ לִי *(mikhra kha-yom et bekhoratkha li)* "sell me your firstborn rights this very day." As the story continues we will see that Jacob's actions (when he fools Isaac into thinking that he is Esau) will not be honored by Abraham's God. There will be a series of severe setbacks to Jacob's life (Laban's dealings with him) which will look remarkably similar to and as dishonest as Jacob's dealings with Esau. Jacob will ultimately be blessed, but certainly not with the blessings he believed he could steal from his brother. Isaac and God had a much greater blessing in store for him – one prepared for him that did not need to be stolen. But Jacob did not know that at the moment.

**Despising Birthright**

The Hebrew root word connected to the idea of the "birthright" and "being firstborn" is בָּכַר *(bakhar)*. It basically refers to the idea of "being first." While Esau is portrayed as a hard-working man, he is also clearly shown as someone who did not distinguish the spiritual significance of being "firstborn" בְּכֹרָה *(bekhorah)*, from the right of being blessed with a mighty "blessing" בְּרָכָה *(berakhah)* that would come later. To the seemingly unreasonable request of his younger brother, "First sell me your birthright," Esau responds: אָנֹכִי הוֹלֵךְ

10

לָמוּת וְלָמָה־זֶּה לִי בְּכֹרָה (anokhi holekh lamut ve-lama zeh li bekhorah) "I am at the point of death, so of what use is my birthright to me?"

True, Esau was tired and hungry. Still, one who has a high esteem for his status as the firstborn will not give up this high status for simple food. The story is clear: when Jacob finally served Esau לֶחֶם וּנְזִיד עֲדָשִׁים (lechem u-nezid adashim) "bread and lentil stew" Esau simply ate and went away. In so doing, the text of Genesis 25:34b says, וַיִּבֶז עֵשָׂו אֶת־הַבְּכֹרָה (va-yivez Esav et ha-bekhorah) "so Esau spurned the birthright." The verb בָּזָה (bazah) has a connotation of "being careless" or "having contempt" – despising something as useless.

## Esau's Marriages

As the story in Genesis 26:6-33 continues, it describes a severe famine in Isaac's time, just as in the time of Abraham. The text then makes a brief but poignant remark that when Esau was forty years old (which signifies the age of full maturity) he took Judith, daughter of Beeri the Hittite, and Basemath, daughter of Elon the Hittite, to be his wives. Both of these women were to become a source of real emotional distress for both Isaac and Rebekah. The Hebrew phrase used to describe this distress in the original text is מֹרַת רוּחַ (morat ruach). It literally means "bitterness of spirit."

The letter ת (tav) replaces ה (hey) at the end of the word מֹרָה (morah), which means "bitterness." The reason is that this term comes before the word for "spirit" רוּחַ (ruach), which causes a state of smikhut here. Smikhut is a Hebrew grammatical situation that arises from a combination of nouns and can articulate possession. It is similar to the possessive function of the word "of" in the English language. Hence, "bitterness of spirit." So Esau's marriages were not a blessing to his family. While the Edomites would be blessed and protected by Israel's God because of His concern and promised blessing to Esau, they can still cause a lot of pain. This statement speaks loudly to later Israelite readers of Genesis. They should not be surprised that Edomites were historically, and still were in their time, a cause of "bitter stress." Just as their matriarchs brought "bitterness" to Isaac and Rebekah, their descendants (the Edomites) would bring bitterness and distress on Israel.

## The Stolen Blessing

Sibling rivalry is a central motif of the Book of Genesis: Cain and Abel, Isaac and Ishmael, Jacob and Esau, Rachel and Leah, and finally, Joseph and his brothers. Sibling rivalry also plays a central role in human conflict. It begins with a very simple desire – the desire to have what your brother has, or even to be what your brother is. Such coveting and craving would one day be forbidden by the Ten Words/Commandments. Those commandments would later come to underlie the morality of the entire Western world. Chapter 27 presents one of the most difficult stories of Genesis. It is certainly one of the masterpieces of biblical narrative artistry.

We all know it as the story of the stolen blessing. The "elephant in the room" is that, while the tricking of Isaac was ethically wrong, God's covenant still continued through Jacob, who was truly blessed in the end. We will take time to walk through this story in order to understand exactly what happened and how we should understand this foundational story of Genesis. The deceit of Isaac, the aged and blind son of Abraham by promise, lays at the root of the very birth of God's covenant people, Israel. These stories are full of ironies and unexpected twists, so we should be ready to be surprised. Walter Brueggemann writes:

> The narrator seems unaware of the incongruity that may appear to us: a blessing gotten by deception! While that may be a problem for us, we do better to stay inside the story itself, to perceive that the narrative is simply that way (as is life itself). Settlement of property and inheritance is seldom achieved without coveting and calculation. That is how it is in this family. The story is powerful enough to speak for itself.[1]

---

[1]   Walter Brueggemann, *Genesis: Interpretation: A Bible Commentary for Teaching and Preaching* (Louisville: Westminster John Knox Press, 2010), 229.

The story begins by stating that Isaac was old, and his eyes were dim, so that he could not see. When Isaac began to ponder his death (vs. 2),[2] he determined, without further delay, to give his blessing (as was traditionally done) to his firstborn and favorite son – Esau. Most of this narrative makes very little sense to many modern people, as we ascribe virtually no value to the paternal blessing of the firstborn son. However, this story, and naturally the characters in the story, treat the blessing very seriously. It can be stolen, just as anything of value can be stolen. This concept should challenge us to rethink our idea of blessing, and to move away from seeing it as something spiritual or theoretical rather than something real and, in fact, very tangible.

"Isaac called his oldest son Esau" וַיִּקְרָא אֶת־עֵשָׂו בְּנוֹ הַגָּדֹל *(va-yikrah et Esav beno ha-gadol)*. Esau answered him with the typical הִנֵּנִי *(hineni)* "Here I am" refrain. It is likely that the text here recalls a similar triple refrain in the binding of Isaac (Gen. 22.1, 7, 11), where Isaac's own father Abraham had answered with the same word. This textual similarity is arguably an indication that the narrator seeks to align the ancient readers' and hearers' sympathy with Esau, rather than with Jacob (although the expression is a common one).

Isaac told Esau that he was now old and had been considering his own passing, not knowing when he would die. We read in Genesis 27:3-4:

וְעַתָּה שָׂא־נָא כֵלֶיךָ תֶּלְיְךָ וְקַשְׁתֶּךָ וְצֵא הַשָּׂדֶה וְצוּדָה לִּי צֵידָה

*Take your gear, your quiver and bow, and go out into the open and hunt me some game. (Gen. 27:3)*

וַעֲשֵׂה־לִי מַטְעַמִּים כַּאֲשֶׁר אָהַבְתִּי וְהָבִיאָה לִּי וְאֹכֵלָה בַּעֲבוּר תְּבָרֶכְךָ נַפְשִׁי בְּטֶרֶם אָמוּת

---

[2]   Isaac was wrong about the nearness of his death. Jacob and Esau did not bury their father until decades later at the age of 180. (Gen. 35:29)

13

*Then prepare a dish for me such as I like, and bring it to me to eat, so that I may give you my innermost blessing before I die." (Gen. 27:4)*

Isaac chooses the timing of bestowing the firstborn blessing very carefully. This is not a spur-of-the-moment decision. As we have already seen, Isaac had a special fondness for Esau כִּי־צַיִד בְּפִיו *(ki tsayid be-fiv)* "because he had a taste for wild game" or, more literally, "for hunting was in his mouth" (Gen. 25:28). So here Isaac sends Esau out to hunt and to bring back the food he desires Esau to prepare for him. There is something precious that Isaac and Esau are anticipating here: the son is feeding the father; the father is blessing the son. Isaac states that he wants the blessing to be full, heartfelt, and thorough – the concepts that are most likely behind the Hebrew phrase תְּבָרֶכְךָ נַפְשִׁי *(tevarekh'kha nafshi)* which literally means something like "my soul/being will bless you."

It is here, in verse 5, that the plan of Isaac and Esau comes undone. Rebekah, who favored her younger son, Jacob, was eavesdropping on their conversation and was persuaded that she needed to act quickly. It is striking that Rebekah did not refer to the motivation for her actions (or at least they are not recorded). Most likely they were rooted in God's words to her when she was pregnant:

שְׁנֵי גֹיִים בְּבִטְנֵךְ וּשְׁנֵי לְאֻמִּים מִמֵּעַיִךְ יִפָּרֵדוּ וּלְאֹם מִלְאֹם יֶאֱמָץ וְרַב יַעֲבֹד צָעִיר:

*"Two nations are in your womb, two separate peoples shall issue from your body; one people shall be mightier than the other, and the older shall serve the younger." (Gen. 25:23)*

Since the texts in chapters 25 and 27 were meant to be read together, not separately, it may be safe to assume that this earlier statement (Gen. 25:23) is not repeated here explicitly because it was presumed to be understood as related to Rebekah's decision. We previously discussed the ambiguity of the phrase וְרַב יַעֲבֹד צָעִיר *(ve-rav yaavod tsair)* "the greater will serve the younger." The consequences are by no means clear. There are essentially two schools of thought as to whether Rebekah did something good by acting with holy zeal, thus forcing history to go "God's way," or whether what she (and Jacob) did was actually evil. Certainly it subsequently caused much pain and suffering to all involved. After all, Jacob was never mentioned as seeing his mother alive again. Astonishingly, she literally invoked upon herself any curse that may rightly have befallen the guilty party in such a questionable transaction (Gen. 27:13).

If Rebekah was right in what she did, then her actions could be compared to Moses' wife Zipporah, who saved her husband's life from God's severe judgement when she circumcised their child (Ex. 4:25). If the view is taken that Rebekah was not right, then her actions could be compared to those of Sarah, when she encouraged Abraham to have relations with Hagar, her servant, in order to ensure that God's promise would not become void. But again, in such interpretations we are not being led by the story itself. It does not seem very concerned to explain the wrongness or rightness of Rebekah's actions here. Rather, the story is about the manifestation of God's mighty promises (and yes, there are more blessings than one) in the context of an intense and true-to-life family drama.

When Esau went out to the field to hunt, his mother quickly sprang into action by telling Jacob about the timing of Isaac's intention to bless Esau. She then implored Jacob to do exactly as she directed, instructing him to go to the flock and to bring to her two choice young lambs, promising that she will then prepare and cook them exactly as his father likes. "Once that is accomplished, you will take it to your father and he will bless you before he dies," said Rebekah to Jacob (Gen. 27:5-10). Jacob expressed some serious doubts about his mother's plan. We read in Genesis 27:11-13:

וַיֹּאמֶר יַעֲקֹב אֶל־רִבְקָה אִמּוֹ הֵן עֵשָׂו אָחִי אִישׁ שָׂעִר וְאָנֹכִי אִישׁ חָלָק

*Jacob answered his mother Rebekah, "But my brother Esau is a hairy man and I am smooth-skinned. (Gen. 27:11)*

The biggest problem to overcome, as far as Jacob was concerned, was that he and Esau were not identical twins — Esau was hairy and Jacob was smooth-skinned. Hebrew phrases such as אִישׁ שָׂעִר *(ish sair)* and אִישׁ חָלָק *(ish chalak)* are forms of expression specifying the kind of אִישׁ *(ish)* "man" or "person" being spoken of. The first literally means "man of hair" or "hairy man" and the second literally "man of (something) smooth" or "smooth man."

אוּלַי יְמֻשֵּׁנִי אָבִי וְהָיִיתִי בְעֵינָיו כִּמְתַעְתֵּעַ וְהֵבֵאתִי עָלַי קְלָלָה וְלֹא בְרָכָה

*If my father touches me, I shall appear to him as a trickster and bring upon myself a curse, not a blessing." (Gen. 27:12)*

Jacob feared that Isaac may lovingly caress him, believing him to be Esau. The verb מָשַׁשׁ *(mashash)* indicates "touch." The use of this word may have been meant to highlight the intimate father-son relationship that Isaac and Esau shared. Jacob is afraid that, if he were to follow his mother's instructions, he may be thought by his father as a "mocker" or "deceiver" מְתַעְתֵּעַ *(metatea)* and be in danger of being cursed by him. The risk is indeed high — either he will receive his father's blessing, which will forever change his life for the better, or it may be the other way around — his father's curse will follow him all the days of his life. Jacob was at loss as to what to do.

The Hebrew word קְלָלָה *(kelalah)* means a "curse," but it has a very interesting meaning which can be better understood if we compare the word to an opposing concept, the Hebrew word כָּבוֹד *(kavod)* meaning "honor" or "glory." This word is connected with the general idea of being כָּבֵד *(kaved)* "being heavy." The opposite of "being heavy" or "honored" is the idea of being "made light of" or "dishonored" and is expressed by the Hebrew word קָלוֹן *(kalon)*. The word we are looking at in this text, קְלָלָה *(kelalah)* is usually translated as "curse," is related and therefore might originally have meant something like "being made light of." The idea is simple — a heavy object is steady, a light object is not. Something heavy is difficult to move from its place, something light can be moved with no real effort. Therefore, the issue here is true-to-life stability and security on every level.

וַתֹּאמֶר לוֹ אִמּוֹ עָלַי קִלְלָתְךָ בְּנִי אַךְ שְׁמַע בְּקֹלִי וְלֵךְ קַח־לִי

*But his mother said to him, "Your curse, my son, be upon me! Just do as I say and go fetch them for me." (Gen. 27:13)*

Rebekah told Jacob not to be concerned about receiving a curse. She was prepared to bear any curse herself, if such were in fact rendered instead of a blessing. Jacob was still young and was expected not to argue with his mother, but to do just what she asked of him. Remember that it seems the story is not being told with the question of ethics in mind. (Did he do right? Did she do wrong?) So we, too, must follow the logic of the story, seeking to grasp the meaning in its original text, free from our modern ideas and concerns. Jacob listened to his mother and their plan was set in motion. The time for Esau to receive his birthright-related blessing was quickly running out. Rebekah then brought to Jacob his brother's festive clothes to wear as he went to Isaac to impersonate Esau. She then covered the bare areas of skin (neck and hands) with the skins of the kids she had used to prepare the food, in order to disguise Jacob to feel like Esau.

Once again Jacob found himself holding a dish of food. This time he will offer it not to Esau, but to his father Isaac. Although the text is, as it is typical for the Book of Genesis, silent about some of the private conversations that must have gone on in the family, it very well may be that Rebekah and Isaac did previously discuss the oracle given by God to Rebekah and the strange events where Esau actually sold his birthright to Jacob for a bowl of soup. If so, it may have been a matter of disagreement between them. Rebekah believed that Isaac should now bless Jacob with the blessing generally belonging to the firstborn, whereas Isaac sought to bless the older son first, as he planned before the birthright sale.

This narrative about Jacob portrays Israel, the patriarch of an entire people in his earthiest and most scandalous appearance in Genesis. It is not edifying in any conventional religious or moral sense. Indeed, if one comes to the narrative with such an agenda, one would find it offensive. But for that very reason, the Jacob narrative is most real, believable and life-like. The Jacob narrative permits candor about the offensiveness of Israel and the resilience of God despite his scandalous actions. As we continue to read the developing story, Jacob approaches his blind father (vs. 18). Jacob greets Isaac with the word "Father." Isaac then asked the most important question: "Which one of my two sons are you?" Isaac answered: "I am Esau, your first-born; I have done as you told me. Please, sit and eat what I hunted, so that you can give me your innermost blessing." Isaac expressed surprise that Esau was able to complete the task so quickly, to which Jacob answered: "Because the Lord your God granted me good fortune" (Gen. 27:18-20).

Even though Isaac sensed that it was Jacob's voice he heard, not Esau's, he chose to ignore this and rely, instead, on his sense of touch. In so doing, he was fooled by Rebekah and Jacob's crafty camouflage, and blessed Jacob in this well-staged identity. In verse 24 the story returns to the time before Isaac rendered the blessing and more conversation between Isaac and Jacob is revealed. At some point Jacob (perhaps remembering his disagreement with Rebekah) asks: "Are you really my son Esau?" Jacob then answers: "I am." Isaac then tells him to serve him the food so that, once consumed, Isaac can proceed with the ceremony of bestowing the blessing. Jacob duly served the food to his father. Isaac beckons Jacob to draw near and kiss him. Upon smelling the clothing of Esau, Isaac was mistakenly convinced that before him there stood his favorite son – Esau (Gen. 27:24-27), so he said:

וַיֹּאמֶר רְאֵה רֵיחַ בְּנִי כְּרֵיחַ שָׂדֶה אֲשֶׁר בֵּרֲכוֹ יהוה

*"Ah, the smell of my son is like the smell of the fields that the LORD has blessed. (Gen. 27:24)*

As we continue to trace Jacob's troublesome life, we will soon encounter his travels to Padan Aram, where Laban, Rebekah's brother, lived. There Jacob will fall in love, serve Laban for seven years, only to find that Laban used the same trick on him as he did on his father Isaac. Leah, the oldest daughter, was given to be his wife, instead of Rachel, whom Jacob loved with all his heart. Jacob will experience at the hands of his uncle Laban the same level of deceit with which he deceived his father, Isaac. The similarities will be stunning, but more about that later.

As we continue in our journey through the life of Jacob, it is imperative that we look carefully at the content of the actual blessing given to Jacob by mistake. We should consider how and why this blessing is different from the second blessing that Isaac gave to Jacob knowingly. This time there will be no case of mistaken identity and every word of blessing to Jacob will be intended for him. We read the exact text of the blessing stolen by Jacob in Genesis 27:28-29:

וְיִתֶּן־לְךָ הָאֱלֹהִים מִטַּל הַשָּׁמַיִם וּמִשְׁמַנֵּי הָאָרֶץ וְרֹב דָּגָן וְתִירֹשׁ

*"May God give you of the dew of heaven and the fat of the earth, abundance of new grain and wine. (Gen. 27:28)*

The basic idea here is that Jacob will not have to work hard in his livelihood, or at least not to an inordinate extent. The earth and the heavens will work for him instead, giving him the fruit of the earth as is symbolized in this text by grain and wine. He will be rich. This part of the blessing did not come to fruition for Jacob at first. Ironically, perhaps, the opposite was true at the start. Jacob had to work fourteen hard years for Laban just to marry Rachel. Later he did become wealthy because God blessed the hard work that he did with care and success. But the wealth and success did not come easy.

יַעַבְדוּךָ עַמִּים וְיִשְׁתַּחוּ לְךָ לְאֻמִּים הֱוֵה גְבִיר לְאַחֶיךָ וְיִשְׁתַּחֲווּ לְךָ בְּנֵי אִמֶּךָ

*Let peoples serve you, and nations bow to you; Be master over your brothers, and let your mother's sons bow to you. (Gen. 27:29)*

Another part of the blessing is stated here explicitly. Jacob will be blessed with enormous power and authority. The nations around Jacob will become his slaves, they will pay homage to his great rule. This part of the stolen blessing also did not seem to come true in his lifetime. As we will see, Jacob struggled with the peoples around him all his life. He was far from the position of power that this blessing described. Addressing the Pharaoh whom Joseph served, Jacob said, "Few and hard have been the years of my life..." (Gen.47:9).

So perhaps Jacob did not get the blessing he had stolen. In fact, it was Jacob as he sought to make peace with his older brother Esau, who called himself his servant or slave and not the other way around (Gen.32:28-20). This is especially clear in what words Jacob's servants were instructed to say to Esau about the animals he encountered, "Your servant Jacob's; they are a gift sent to my lord Esau." Then upon the actual meeting of brothers, Jacob "himself went on ahead and bowed low to the ground seven times until he was near his brother" (Gen.33:3). Another part of this stolen blessing said:

אֹרְרֶיךָ אָרוּר וּמְבָרֲכֶיךָ בָּרוּךְ

*Cursed be they who curse you, blessed they who bless you." (Gen. 27:29)*

It is hardly a surprise that this part of the blessing will not have an immediate fulfillment in the life of Jacob either.

## The Real Blessing

Later the same day, when Rebekah found out that Esau planned to eventually put Jacob to death, Isaac and Rebekah sent their younger son Jacob to Rebekah's brother Laban in Haran. Abraham and his father Terah settled in Haran after leaving Ur of the Chaldees while en route to the Promised Land (Gen. 11:31). It was located in Paddan Aram (the field of Aram in Aramaic). Returning there perhaps constituted a "setback" as far the promises of the covenant are concerned. It did not look like things were going well for the heir of Abraham's covenant. After all, Jacob had to go back to where Abraham his grandfather had come from. There was no visible progress, only visible regress. But, as is often the case, what in our eyes may appear to be "going back" is simply a part of God's plan. In reality, true spiritual progress takes place in times of adversity and struggle.

It is at this precise point, when Jacob is characterized by ultimate weakness (hiding out from the revenge of his furious duped brother), that Isaac blesses Jacob with a different blessing – the blessing that was meant for him. We read the exact text of that second blessing given by Isaac to Jacob in Genesis 28:3-4. All of these words came to full fruition. They promised Jacob that God the Provider will grant him a large number of offspring and that they will have their own Land.

וְאֵל שַׁדַּי יְבָרֵךְ אֹתְךָ וְיַפְרְךָ וְיַרְבֶּךָ וְהָיִיתָ לִקְהַל עַמִּים

*May El Shaddai bless you, make you fertile and numerous, so that you become an assembly of peoples. (Gen. 28:3)*

This particular blessing invokes the name of God as אֵל שַׁדַּי *(El Shaddai)*. As mentioned above, the Hebrew etymology of this special name is not certain. Several theories have been put forward about its meaning. One explains that *El Shaddai* is "God Almighty," a name connected with the Hebrew verb שָׁדַד, meaning "to destroy, despoil." Another theory speaks of "God of the Mountains" – a name connected with the Acadian word *shadau*. It is also quite possible that *El Shaddai*, instead, should be translated as "God the Provider," "God who is Sufficient" or "God the Sufficient One." There are two basic reasons for such interpretations. The word שַׁדַּי *(shaddai)* may be connected with the Hebrew root word for "breast" שַׁד *(shad)*. The female breast is one of the clear symbols of provision for the beginning and the very substance of human life and nourishment. Alternatively, the letter שׁ (shin) may be understood as a prefix that means "then." In this scenario, די (dai) may be taken to mean "sufficiency" which in Hebrew literally means "enough."

The blessing promises וְיַפְרְךָ וְיַרְבֶּךָ (ve-yafrekha ve-yarbekha), that God will "make (Jacob) fertile and numerous." Simply put, it promises him a large number of descendants with the purpose of becoming an "assembly of the peoples" לִקְהַל עַמִּים (li-kehal amim). The verbs are the same ones that were used in Genesis 1:28 when God told Adam and Eve to be "fruitful and multiply" פְּרוּ וּרְבוּ (peru u-revu). Just as we observed a clear connection to the first human being – Adam – in the lives of Noah, Abraham, and Isaac so now we see the same link with Jacob.

וְיִתֶּן־לְךָ אֶת־בִּרְכַּת אַבְרָהָם לְךָ וּלְזַרְעֲךָ אִתָּךְ לְרִשְׁתְּךָ אֶת־אֶרֶץ מְגֻרֶיךָ אֲשֶׁר־נָתַן
אֱלֹהִים לְאַבְרָהָם

*"May He grant the blessing of Abraham to you and your offspring that you may possess the land where you are sojourning, which God assigned to Abraham."* (Gen. 28:4)

This is truly a very different blessing from the first. It does not focus on wealth and power, but rather covenantal continuity is stressed. What is promised to Jacob is only the descendants and the land. This blessing is clearly identified with the blessing of Jacob's grandfather, Abraham himself. Rabbi Jonathan Sacks explained it this way: "Time and again God blesses the patriarchs – but always and only in terms of children and a land. He never promises them 'the richness of the earth,' or that they will 'Rule over their brothers.' Wealth and power have nothing to do with the covenant. They are not part of Israel's destiny."[3]

---

3   Jonathan Sacks, *Not in God's Name: Confronting Religious Violence* (New York: Schocken Books, 2015), 135.

One can wonder, what would have happened if Sarah never suggested to Abraham to ensure the fulfillment of God's promise through Hagar and Ishmael? Also, how would the world look if Jacob never stole the blessing that belonged to Esau? The Hebrew Bible, however, does not encourage us to think in this direction. Instead the Scriptures seek to make sense of our reality, the situation on the ground. The ancient texts give visionary directions for lives of individuals (Genesis) and nations (Exodus) in an imperfect and broken world.

Later, when Jacob grows old, he will bless his son Judah with a special blessing. He will bless a son who comes from the womb of the wife that he ironically loved less, Leah. Judah's blessing is closely connected to the blessing that that was stolen from Esau. It will not pertain to the days of the patriarchs, but to the days of the kings, and even to the "latter days" (Gen. 49:1). This would not be simply the blessing of the patriarchs Abraham, Isaac and Jacob (posterity and land). Instead, this blessing is for the King of Israel. Judah's dynasty was divinely chosen to rule over Israel and the world-at-large (prosperity, strength, rule, and assured protection). In Genesis 49:1, 8-10 we read:

And Jacob called his sons and said, "Come together that I may tell you what is to befall you in the latter days בְּאַחֲרִית הַיָּמִים (be-acharit ha-yamim). You, O Judah יְהוּדָה אַתָּה (Yehudah atah), your brothers shall praise יוֹדוּךָ אַחֶיךָ (yodukha achekha); Your hand shall be on the nape of your foes יָדְךָ בְּעֹרֶף אֹיְבֶיךָ (yadkha be-oref oyvekha); Your father's sons shall bow low to you יִשְׁתַּחֲווּ לְךָ בְּנֵי אָבִיךָ (yishtachavu lekha bene avikha). Judah is a young lion גּוּר אַרְיֵה יְהוּדָה (gur aryah Yehudah)... The scepter shall not depart from Judah לֹא־יָסוּר שֵׁבֶט מִיהוּדָה (lo yasur shevet mi-Yhudah), nor the ruler's staff from between his feet וּמְחֹקֵק מִבֵּין רַגְלָיו (u-mechokek mi-ben raglav); Until that tribute shall come to him and the homage of peoples be his עַד כִּי־יָבֹא שִׁילֹה וְלוֹ יִקְהַת עַמִּים (ad ki yavo shiloh ve-lo yikhat amim)."

In the book of Numbers we read about Balaam who is forced by God to pronounce a blessing upon Israel, which resounds Jacob's words. It becomes clear that Israel's king is destined for victorious rule over the nations in fulfillment of Jacob's blessing to Judah (Num. 24:2-9). It is through this ultimate King of Israel that mankind's return to "the garden of Eden," formerly lost, will eventually be accomplished. This King, unlike Adam, will rule and exercise His God-given responsibility, but without sin (Num. 24:19; Gen. 1:26).

## Jacob's Dream

One of the most famous human encounters with God in the Bible is the dream of "Jacob's Ladder." This immensely significant event took place when Jacob was on the way from Beer Sheva to Haran. Jacob had been on the run from Esau for some time when he came to "a certain place" which, at that time, was unknown. It was, however, destined to become one of the most important religious sites in the world. We are of course talking about Bethel – the House of God. While the precise location of Bethel today is disputed, its significance is not. Significant holy places in the Ancient Near East were not considered chosen by humans, but quite the opposite. In the minds of the people, it was the gods who chose places on earth because of their inherent holiness and uniqueness. Then they revealed their will to the holy men.

We see something similar here at Bethel, and yet, also something very different. Upon reaching this "place," the sun had set and the weary Jacob stopped there to rest for the night. He took a stone and placed it under his head as a pillow and laid down to sleep. During the night something happened that neither he nor his descendants could ever forget. While Jacob slept he had a dream. We read the details in Genesis 28:12-15:

וְהִנֵּה סֻלָּם מֻצָּב אַרְצָה וְרֹאשׁוֹ מַגִּיעַ הַשָּׁמָיְמָה וְהִנֵּה מַלְאֲכֵי אֱלֹהִים עֹלִים וְיֹרְדִים בּוֹ

*"… a stairway was set on the ground and its top reached to the sky, and angels of God were going up and down on it." (Gen. 28:12)*

Brueggemann says: "The framework of the journey (vv. 10–11) is not very important except that the event happens "between places," where nothing unusual was expected. Jacob's encounter with God happened between safe, identifiable places, but here, everything is uncertain. Suffice to say at this point, that this "non-place" is transformed by a visitation from God into a crucially important place. The transformation takes place during sleep, when Jacob has lost control of his destiny… in the process, this "non-person" (i.e., exiled, threatened) is transformed by the coming of God to a person crucial for the promise."[4]

The fivefold repetition of the term מָקוֹם *(makom)* "place" between vs. 11 and 17 demands our attention. This leads us to ask what was the significance of this *place*? The "non-place" becomes *"the place,"* and the "non-person" becomes *"the person."* The marvel is the grace of God which makes this miraculous encounter a reality.

Since we don't really know what "Jacob's ladder" looked like, we should entertain at least a few possibilities when trying to visualize it. One can visualize a traditional portable wooden ladder we use today for climbing hard to reach places. Hypothetically, something like that could have appeared in Jacob's vision. But what is more likely is that he saw a stone staircase. Perhaps something that looked more like an ancient Ziggurat. This was a common sacred structure in the ancient Near East, a hill with long stairs leading up to the deity situated on the top of those ascending series of stones.

The word סֻלָּם *(sulam)* is difficult to translate accurately because this is the only passage in Hebrew Bible where it is used. Thus "ramp" and "stairway" have been justifiably suggested in addition to "ladder" as possible translations. What is important is that this "ladder" was

---

4    Brueggemann, *Genesis: Interpretation*, 242.

set up on earth and its top reached heaven. The most important revelation that Jacob must grasp in this dream is that the God of heaven is truly involved with what is happening on earth. Jacob's eyes were opened to see the traffic moving between heaven and earth, which could not be seen with the natural, naked eye. Angels of God (His obedient servants/ messengers) were ascending and descending to fulfill God's will on Earth. In Psalm 91:10-11 this heaven/earth connection is stated clearly: "There will no evil befall you, neither will any plague come near to your tent. For He will give His angels charge over you, to keep you in all thy ways."

It is interesting that when Jacob returns to Canaan, the Promised Land, the LORD appears to him once again at Bethel (Gen. 35:1), where an altar is built and the covenant is reiterated along the lines of the covenant with Isaac and Abraham (35:12). The angels of God meet him when leaving the land (Gen. 28:12) and when he returns (Gen. 32:2), forming a literary *inclusio* (everything that happens with him in exile happens between these two angel-related visions/dreams).

While Jacob was not expecting a spiritual encounter at this point, but was concerned only for his own survival, the God of Abraham and Isaac appeared to this deceitful fugitive. In His grace and covenant mercy, God made Himself known to Jacob. The first step was to enable Jacob to comprehend something that he had not previously known.

**The Resource of Heaven**

The God of his forefathers speaks to Jacob in his dream and His words are incredible:

וְהִנֵּה יהוה נִצָּב עָלָיו וַיֹּאמַר אֲנִי יהוה אֱלֹהֵי אַבְרָהָם אָבִיךָ וֵאלֹהֵי יִצְחָק הָאָרֶץ
אֲשֶׁר אַתָּה שֹׁכֵב עָלֶיהָ לְךָ אֶתְּנֶנָּה וּלְזַרְעֶךָ

26

*And the LORD was standing beside him and He said, "I am the LORD, the God of your father Abraham and the God of Isaac: the ground on which you are lying I will assign to you and to your offspring. (Gen. 28:13)*

In Brueggemann's words: "The element in the narrative that surprises Jacob and seems incredible to us is not the religious phenomenon of appearance. It is the wonder, mystery, and shock that this God should be present in such a decisive way to this exiled one. The miracle is the way this sovereign God binds himself to this treacherous fugitive. The event is told as an inexplicable experience. It cannot be assessed by any comparisons or norms outside itself."[5]

From time to time deities were known to appear to holy men of the Ancient Near East, but this God was unusual. He made self-binding promises. The LORD confirmed that the second blessing that Isaac gave to Jacob could be fully relied upon (unlike the first one that was stolen). The same God who spoke to Jacob's grandfather Abraham, and his own father Isaac, is now addressing him directly. God's message was unequivocal: Jacob and his descendants would be given the very land upon which he was now sleeping. God's goodness and promises to him and his forefathers must not be doubted.

The time would come when Jacob and his descendants *would* possess this land. The fact that this happened in a dream when Jacob was, by definition, fully passive is very significant. What God said and did had absolutely nothing to do with any manipulation on the part of Jacob. This encounter was instigated by God alone and it was He who was fully in charge of all the events that took place. Curiously, God provided Eve for Adam by causing him to sleep deeply. This part of the story should also remind the readers that Abraham, as well, fell asleep when God made the covenant with him. Now the pattern repeats. The Earth is not left to its own resources, and heaven is not a remote self-contained realm for the gods. Heaven is intrinsically tied up with earth, and earth finally may count on the

---

[5]    Brueggemann, *Genesis: Interpretation*, 242.

resources of heaven. The LORD God is connected with Israel and even with the very place where Jacob slept.

וְהָיָה זַרְעֲךָ כַּעֲפַר הָאָרֶץ וּפָרַצְתָּ יָמָּה וָקֵדְמָה וְצָפֹנָה וָנֶגְבָּה וְנִבְרֲכוּ בְךָ כָּל־מִשְׁפְּחֹת הָאֲדָמָה וּבְזַרְעֶךָ

*"Your descendants shall be as the dust of the earth; you shall spread out to the west and to the east, to the north and to the south. All the families of the earth shall bless themselves by you and your descendants." (Gen. 28:14)*

According to the promise of God, Jacob will not simply be blessed with children as his forefathers were. It is important to see that he will be blessed with an immeasurable number of children. Not only that, but Jacob and his offspring will become a blessing to all "peoples/families of the earth" מִשְׁפְּחֹת הָאֲדָמָה *(mishpechot ha-adamah).* Here the word for "earth" אֲדָמָה *(adamah)* is etymologically connected with "Adam" אָדָם *(adam).* It is not simply a promise of well-being for Israel, but a promise of well-being for the nations through Israel.

**God's Guarantee**

God continued to speak to Jacob:

וְהִנֵּה אָנֹכִי עִמָּךְ וּשְׁמַרְתִּיךָ בְּכֹל אֲשֶׁר־תֵּלֵךְ וַהֲשִׁבֹתִיךָ אֶל־הָאֲדָמָה הַזֹּאת כִּי לֹא אֶעֱזָבְךָ עַד אֲשֶׁר אִם־עָשִׂיתִי אֵת אֲשֶׁר־דִּבַּרְתִּי לָךְ

*"Remember, I am with you: I will protect you wherever you go and will bring you back to this land. I will not leave you until I have done what I have promised you." (Gen. 28:15)*

As the story of Israel builds, the parallels between Jacob and Joseph (although chronologically still in the future) should not be overlooked. Both Jacob and Joseph were younger brothers whose future was predicted by dreams. Both were exiled because of conflicts with their brothers. These conflicts were such that there was a clear intent to kill, both in Jacob's and in Joseph's stories. In the

28

end both reconciled with their brothers. They both died in Egypt and were buried in the Promised Land.

Like the promise to Abraham (also given in a dream), Jacob's promise receives full clarification in a dream. We see three distinct promises: 1) God's own continual presence, 2) God's own protection everywhere, and 3) Jacob's eventual return to the Promised Land.

*First – God's Presence*: This is one of the most important themes throughout the Holy Scriptures – the idea that the God of Heaven will be "with us, with His people" and in this case with this fugitive on the run – Jacob. What can be counted as a better assurance of avoiding life's danger than the constant presence of the most powerful being anywhere – the God of Abraham, Isaac and now Jacob?! It is amazing that God, who spoke to Jacob from the top of the ramp, promised that his own personal presence would remain with him. God was not going to merely send His representatives (angels) to be with this heir of the Abrahamic covenant. So important was Jacob to God, that He stated these astounding words: אָנֹכִי עִמָּךְ *(anokhi imakh)* "I am with you."

*Second – God's Protection:* God promised to protect Jacob in all his travels. Of course this protection would far outlast Jacob's personal wanderings. Whether Jacob remains in the Promised Land or departs from it would not matter – he would be protected wherever he goes because God's personal presence would guard him. What an astounding promise! In the ancient world, the gods were connected to particular lands/territories. In most people's minds no single God ruled supreme all over the world. People could leave the domain of one god and enter the domain of another. This ancient worldview of gods and lands was something similar to our understanding of criminally-run cities of today, where all neighborhoods are clearly delineated and covered by a particular gang. If you are under the protection of a powerful gang in one place, such protection is not guaranteed in another area. Here God tells Jacob that it makes no difference where his travels take him. God will protect him absolutely anywhere, even in the pagan Padan-Aram from which his grandfather journeyed to settle in Canaan.

***Third – Jacob's Return:*** Not only did God promise Jacob that he could count on His personal presence to protect him anywhere, but also that Jacob's exile was temporary. God would bring him home. "The search for a bride" in Padan-Aram was clearly presented as an excuse for what is actually a flight for Jacob's life, an excuse engineered by Rebekah with her melodramatic complaint about paganism in Canaan (27:46)[6] – even if that also has parallels in the earlier stories of the family. One day Jacob's exile would come to an end and he would be able to return home to the Land of Promise. God, Himself, guaranteed that, and now Jacob was assured of it. The Lord of the Covenant would not rest until all the words of His promise became a reality. The day would come when Jacob would no longer be a fugitive from Esau's justice.

Decades later, peace, forgiveness and brotherly love would prevail, and Jacob and Esau would bury their father Isaac together in the Land of Promise (Gen. 35:29). Jacob's exile may be compared to the time the Israelites wandered in the wilderness after their exodus from Egypt. They were waiting for the Lord to come through on His words of promise as well. The message of God's story is clear. Just as God can be trusted to do what He promised to Jacob, He can also be trusted to fulfill what He promised regarding Jacob's descendants – deliverance of the children of Israel from Egypt.

## Jacob's Vow

When Jacob awoke from his sleep he said to himself, יֵשׁ יהוה בַּמָּקוֹם הַזֶּה וְאָנֹכִי לֹא יָדָעְתִּי *(yesh YHWH ba-makom ha-zeh ve-anokhi lo yadati)*, which translated means "The LORD is in this place, and I did not know." As Jacob was awakened to the realization of the significance

---

6    Robert Alter, *Genesis: Translation and Commentary* (New York: W.W. Norton, 1998): 147.

of the place where he unintentionally slept that night, his language reflected the awesome truth that had become profoundly real to him. "Is this not a house of God?" אֵין זֶה כִּי אִם־בֵּית אֱלֹהִים *(eyn zeh ki im bet Elohim)*; "this is the gate to heaven!" זֶה שַׁעַר הַשָּׁמָיִם *(zeh shaar ha-shamaim)*. Though prior to Jacob's encounter with God this place was known as Luz, Jacob re-named it Bethel – meaning "House of God" – setting up a stone as a memorial of the revelation he received.

The setting up of stones as memorials seems to have been a way to mark significant times and places (a practice which continues even today). This practice will be repeated by many Israelite leaders to commemorate significant events in their lives as well. Moses, in particular in Exodus 24, will set up 12 stones, representing each of the Israelite tribes, as a sign of their full participation in the covenant with the LORD God at Mt. Sinai. Jacob responded to God with his own very significant vow, saying that if LORD keeps His three promises (to be with him and keep him safe, to sustain him with food and clothing, and to bring him home to his father's house) then he, Jacob, will honor God:

וְהָיָה יהוה לִי לֵאלֹהִים

*The LORD shall be my God. (Gen. 28:21)*

In the ancient times the main question was not whether or not God existed, as it is today for many people. The issue in ancient times also was not which interpretation (religion) of that God was the correct one. Instead, the ancients asked one principal question: Which god (in this god-congested universe) should/will be my god? Or which deity should I be in covenant with and serve? Jacob decides that, if יהוה *(YHWH)* "the LORD" keeps His word, then he will choose Him (presumably Him alone) to be his God, saying: וְהָיָה יהוה לִי לֵאלֹהִים *(ve-haya YHWH li l-Elohim)* "The LORD will be my God."

וְהָאֶבֶן הַזֹּאת אֲשֶׁר־שַׂמְתִּי מַצֵּבָה יִהְיֶה בֵּית אֱלֹהִים

*And this stone, which I have set up as a pillar, shall be God's abode. (Gen. 28:22a)*

While it is of no special significance here, it is a good place to note that the word אֶבֶן (*even*), preceded by its definite article -ה (*ha-*), is grammatically feminine (translated it means "stone"). In Hebrew, as in many other languages, the feminine gender of a word does not necessarily mean the object has some distinct feminine qualities. The feminine gender is just the grammatical form for reasons that are not always clear. The word is, therefore, being used with feminine demonstrative pronoun זאת (*zot*) "this" and not the masculine one זֶה (*zeh*). By the way, Hebrew has no neuter gender, so all objects (animate or inanimate) will be either masculine or feminine. It is interesting to note that Jacob does not say that the stone that he is setting up as a memorial will be "a sign" of where the House of God will be, but that the stone itself will be the house of God (perhaps an idiom used at the time to denote a site of worship).

Jacob makes another promise:

וְכֹל אֲשֶׁר תִּתֶּן־לִי עַשֵּׂר אֲעַשְּׂרֶנּוּ לָךְ:

*And of all that You give me, I will set aside a tithe for You. (Gen. 28:22b)*

Jacob makes his conditional commitment concrete by promising to set aside a tithe of everything that the LORD God gives him. As Walter Brueggemann says, "Jacob the trickster is now bound to this God who presides over all the trickery yet to come in the narrative," notably with Laban-related stories.[7] Genesis has described Jacob as אִישׁ תָּם (*ish tam*), sometimes translated as "a simple man" or "a peaceful man," but better understood as "whole" or "blameless" or arguably even "single-minded" (Gen. 25:27). It is interesting that the prophet Micah associates Jacob with truth – "You give truth to Jacob, kindness to Abraham" (Micah 7:20). Jacob's life embodies the fact that truth must be fought for with determination. It rarely comes without a struggle and the pain of experience.[8]

7    Brueggemann, *Genesis: Interpretation*, 248.
8    See Jonathan Sacks, *Covenant & Conversation: a Weekly Reading of the Jewish Bible*. Genesis: The Book of Beginnings (New Milford, CT: Maggid Books & The Orthodox Union, 2009): 225-227.

Truth was learned by Jacob. He learned it through pain acquired through his dangerous journeys and owned by him (though imperfectly) through his vows. What is that truth? Jacob does not belong to himself or even to his family, but to the LORD God who bound Himself to Jacob by His promises. Jacob's end response is fully appropriate – from everything that God gives him, he will give a tenth portion to God. The imperfect vow that Jacob gave has successfully led him to "sustained, disciplined worship."[9] There is hope for Jacob; there is hope for Israel; there is hope for the nations of the world.

## An Imperfect Family

The story of Jacob arriving in the Haran area begins in Genesis 29 and immediately places us, as hearers of the story, next to a well, not far from Laban's house and land. A large stone covered the opening of the water delivery system in such a way that it was rolled away only when the flock of all the owners living in the area were assembled. Jacob inquired about Laban from the people that were at the well. The shepherds pointed out to Jacob that Rachel, a shepherdess and Laban's daughter, was in fact approaching the well with her flock. Jacob meets Rachel and breaks into tears. Jacob moves the rock to give water to her flock. It is interesting that both his ability to move the rock and Rachel's work in the family (shepherdess) speak of strength of both character and body. In response Rachel ran to her father Laban and together she and Laban ran back to Jacob. Jacob leveled with Laban about his troubles with Esau (Gen. 29:13). to which Laban interestingly responds in the words of Adam: עַצְמִי וּבְשָׂרִי אָתָּה *(atsmi u-vesari atah)*, which means "You are my bone and my flesh!" (Gen. 2:23; 29:14). As the readers discover from the rest of the story, Jacob has met his match. Laban would turn out to be as manipulative and deceptive as Jacob. Behind Laban's warm Eastern-style family welcome lay the self-seeking, manipulative heart of an impossible-to-satisfy, ungrateful man.

---

9   Brueggemann, *Genesis: Interpretation*, 248.

## What Goes Around...

Laban had two daughters. The older daughter's name was Leah, of whom it is said that her eyes were weak, and a younger daughter Rachel, of whom it was said that she was very beautiful. So when Laban told Jacob to name the price for his work in Laban's family business, Jacob did not hesitate and said that he will work for seven full years to get Rachel to become his wife. Time passed and Jacob's years of service were up so Laban agreed to have a wedding feast. Nothing alerted Jacob to an impending disappointment. After the feast, when it was already very dark, Laban led Leah instead of the promised Rachel to Jacob's tent. The two consummated their union but, when the sun rose and first rays of light began to break into the tent, Jacob realized how Laban and Leah tricked him. Next to him was a sister-like figure he had perhaps grown to love, care for, and respect as a relative. But his beloved Rachel was not in sight.

When Jacob confronted Laban about this, Laban said that it was not their custom to marry off a younger daughter before the older. In one of the later rabbinic midrashim (creative interpretive rethinking of the biblical text) we read the following imagined reenactment of Jacob-Leah conversation: "Said he [Jacob] to her [Leah]: 'You are a deceiver and the daughter of a deceiver!' 'Is there a teacher without pupils?' she retorted. 'Did not your father call you Esau, and you answered him! So did you too call me and I answered you!'" (Midrash Rabbah, Bereishit 70:19) There is no doubt that in this story Jacob is being treated by Laban and Leah exactly how he and his mother Rebekah treated Esau and Isaac. What goes around, as they say, comes around.

## A Faithless Competition

After the wedding week was completed Laban gave Rachel to Jacob as his second wife in exchange for another seven years of work. Jacob probably cared for both women as a good husband would, but he clearly loved the younger daughter more (Gen. 29:30). Rachel knew it and so did Leah. In the Hebrew Bible "loved less" can be expressed as "unloved" or even "hated." The LORD who promised to be with Jacob at all times does something that Jacob and Rachel could not understand. The narrative that establishes the origins of Jacob's family begins with barrenness, just as was the case with Abraham and Sarah, and Isaac and Rebekah. He opened up Leah's womb, but closed the womb of Rachel. The text says very clearly that this was so because "the LORD saw that Leah was unloved" (Gen. 29:31). Thus, the story of Jacob introduces the themes of injustice and love. This love will be a characteristic of Jacob and will one day become extremely important for the nation of Israel as well. Sacks writes:

> Nowhere in Genesis do we read that Abraham loved Sarah. Once we hear that Isaac loved Rebekah. Three times we read that Jacob loved Rachel, and three times that he loved Joseph. The Hebrew Bible is a book of love: love God with all your heart, soul and might (Deut. 6:5); love your neighbor as yourself (Lev. 19:18); love the stranger (Lev. 19:34). But love is not unproblematic. Given to one but not another, to one more than another, it creates tensions that can turn to violence. More than any other character in Genesis, Jacob loves, but the result is conflict between Leah and Rachel and between Joseph and his brothers. The message of Genesis is that love is necessary but not sufficient. You also need sensitivity to those who feel unloved.[10]

The firstborn of Jacob is Reuben and, as the narrative continues in predicable fashion, we find out that in time other sons of Jacob would outshine Reuben. Being born first does not equal automatic entitlement to true leadership in Israel. To lead one must have moral courage, a selfless attitude, and a life marked by a true ability to repent (change of actions). The time will come when both Joseph, Jacob's youngest son, and Judah, a son of the woman less loved, will demonstrate their leadership character traits. Leah gave Jacob four sons in a row: Reuben, Simeon, Levi and Judah. Each time she gave a name to a son, she did it in a way that reflected her deep desire to

---

[10]  Sacks, *Not In God's Name*, 145.

be loved by Jacob as much (or more) as Rachel. We will take a closer look at names later. Leah's feelings of being loved less, unloved, and even hated were the defining factor in her life. It would be a mistake to think that this insecurity was not passed on to her children in the form of disdain towards Joseph, the firstborn of Rachel, supremely loved by Jacob.

Judah seemed to be Leah's last son after a period of several births (Gen. 29:35), but her misguided passion and methodology to get into the center of Jacob's love did not stop. She was competing against Rachel. She, the unloved one, desperately wanted to be loved by Jacob. Rachel's envy towards her sister reached a high point when, in the depth of her despair, she demanded of Jacob to give her children, too, (Gen. 30:1) as if he was withholding this from her. Naturally this placed even more strain on a difficult relationship between Jacob and his first love, Rachel. Jacob lashed back at Rachel. Rachel gave Jacob a concubine who bore him Dan and Naphtali in the name of Rachel. Judging from the names she gave, envy and a sense of not-being-loved-enough by Jacob's God defined her life just as it defined Leah's. One can only imagine how Jacob struggled with both of them being part of one family.

It was now Leah's turn to hit back at her chief rival. Persuaded that Judah was her last son, she offered her servant as a concubine to Jacob as well. As a result, Gad and Asher were born in the name of Leah. So the child-bearing and child-counting race continued. Leah was still in the lead, but neither the winner nor the looser felt loved. The story of manipulation on the part of Israel's matriarchs goes into the next scene. It moves from the domain of surrogate births to herbal therapy. In Genesis 30:14 we read that Leah's oldest son found a rare root plant that was believed to increase fertility in women (mandrake plant). Rachel bargained with Leah, offering her Jacob for the night in exchange for some of the plant. This is very similar to how Jacob bargained with Esau for his birthright at a time of desperate need. Rachel did not get pregnant soon after this, but Leah went on to give Jacob two more sons – Issachar and Zebulun

– and one daughter – Dinah. The mandrakes did not work (at least they did not work for Rachel), but God remembered Rachel, had compassion on her, finally opened her womb, and she gave birth to Joseph. Later, Jacob would formally count both sons of Joseph's Egyptian wife (Ephraim and Manasseh) as his own during his blessing, preferring the younger (Manasseh) and giving him the largest portion of land from all the twelve tribes.

## Jacob's Family

The sons of Jacob from both Leah and Rachel (whether born by them or in their names) are:

| Leah | Rachel |
|------|--------|
| 1. Rueben | 1. Dan |
| 2. Simeon | 2. Naphtali |
| 3. Levy | 3. Joseph |
| 4. Judah | 4. Benjamin |
| 5. Gad | |
| 6. Asher | |
| 7. Issachar | |
| 8. Zebulun | |

רְאוּבֵן **Reuben** כִּי־רָאָה יהוה בְּעָנְיִי *"Because the LORD saw my poverty"* *(Gen. 29:32)*

שִׁמְעוֹן **Simeon** כִּי־שָׁמַע יהוה כִּי־שְׂנוּאָה אָנֹכִי *"Because the LORD heard that I was unloved/hated"* *(Gen. 29:33)*

לֵוִי **Levy** הַפַּעַם יִלָּוֶה אִישִׁי אֵלַי *"This time my man will accompany me"* *(Gen. 29:34)*

יְהוּדָה **Judah** הַפַּעַם אוֹדֶה אֶת־יהוה *"This time I will praise the LORD."* *(Gen. 29:35)*

דָּן **Dan** דָּנַנִּי אֱלֹהִים *"God vindicated me."* *(Gen. 30:6)*

37

נַפְתָּלִי **Naphtali** נִפְתַּלְתִּי עִם־אֲחֹתִי *"I wrestled with my sister." (Gen. 30:8)*

גָּד **Gad** בְּגָד *"In the luck/fortune." (Gen. 30:11)*

אָשֵׁר **Asher** בְּאָשְׁרִי כִּי אִשְּׁרוּנִי בָּנוֹת *"In happiness, because the girls (will deem me?) happy/blessed." (Gen. 30:13)*

יִשָּׂשׂכָר **Issachar** נָתַן אֱלֹהִים שְׂכָרִי אֲשֶׁר־נָתַתִּי שִׁפְחָתִי לְאִישִׁי *"God gave me my reward because I gave my maidservant to my man." (Gen. 30:18)*

זְבֻלוּן **Zebulun** זְבָדַנִי אֱלֹהִים אֹתִי זֶבֶד טוֹב הַפַּעַם יִזְבְּלֵנִי אִישִׁי *"God bestowed upon me a good gift; this time my man will honor me (make me his legitimate wife)." (Gen. 30:20)*

יוֹסֵף **Joseph** יֹסֵף יהוה לִי בֵּן אַחֵר *"God will/ may add me another son." (Gen. 30:24)*

בִּנְיָמִין **Benjamin** בִּנְיָמִין *"Son of my strength/ right hand"* – changed from Rachel's original name בֶּן־אוֹנִי *"Son of my sorrow" (Gen. 35:18)*

The story of the birthright bought and the blessing stolen by Jacob, as well as the stories of manipulation by Leah and Rachel, show that the origins of Israel as a family were far from perfect. Jacob's family was very much like Jacob himself: flawed. Yet the wonder of it all is that the narrator, far from hiding these facts, parades them to the readers/hearers instead. This is the point. The people in these stories are imperfect, but God who chose to do His will through them, He is perfect! They do not "deserve" the benefits of His commitment and covenantal love, but the LORD God enters into covenant relations with these imperfect sons and daughters of Adam. There is hope. All these stories are really not about these characters, but about the character of God.

# Jacob's Exodus

Genesis 30:25 informs the reader that after Rachel gave birth to Joseph, Jacob asked Laban to allow him to return to his father's home and his own land. Laban sought to slow down and defraud Jacob through further trickery, but all his cunning amounts to nothing. Jacob continued to prosper (his flocks grew exponentially) under the most unpromising of circumstances, as we find out later, all because of God's revelation through a dream (Gen. 31:11-13). As Jacob prepared to return and face Esau, God prospered him. His newly found prosperity is described in Genesis 30:43 as follows:

וַיִּפְרֹץ הָאִישׁ מְאֹד מְאֹד וַיְהִי־לוֹ צֹאן רַבּוֹת וּשְׁפָחוֹת וַעֲבָדִים וּגְמַלִּים וַחֲמֹרִים׃

*So the man grew exceedingly prosperous, and came to own large flocks, maidservants and menservants, camels and asses. (Gen. 30:43)*

The root word פָּרַץ *(parats)* is used here to describe Jacob's growth in wealth. It carries a meaning of "breaking through," "breaking away" and "spreading wide," and is used here in connection with breaking away from the situation of being "limited," "restricted" and "bound." So when God's blessing on Jacob is described, it is depicted in terms of "breaking away" from the limitations placed upon his life, both by his own prior actions toward Esau and Laban's wicked enslavement of Jacob and his unwillingness to set him free.[11]

In Hebrew, we commonly see repetition of the same words used as a way of emphasis. Here, Jacob's prosperity is described as מְאֹד מְאֹד *(me'od me'od)*, which translated means "very-very" or "exceedingly." This repetitive phrase מְאֹד מְאֹד *(me'od me'od)* also appears in the promise to Abraham (Gen. 17:2, 6 twice!) and again in Ex. 1:7 showing that this language refers to the promise given and fulfilled with both Abraham and Jacob and yet to be fulfilled in the future in

---

[11] The same verb is used in Gen. 28:14 promising that he would "expand" in all directions with his seed. In Ex. 1:12 it describes the multiplication of Israel while oppressed by Pharaoh.

Egypt. The use of the פָּרַץ (parats) verb and מְאֹד מְאֹד (me'od me'od) repetition refers to the same promise.

Word endings in Hebrew often determine whether nouns are masculine or feminine. In Hebrew, the suffix וֹת- (-ot) is a plural feminine ending, while יִם- (-im) is plural masculine. We see these endings in words like שְׁפָחוֹת (shefachot) "maidservants" (feminine plural), and וַעֲבָדִים וּגְמַלִּים וַחֲמֹרִים (va-avadim u-gemalim va-chamorim) "and servants and camels and donkeys" (plural masculine endings).

Jacob heard that Laban's sons were talking behind his back, saying that he had taken what belonged to their father and prospered from that capital. At about the same time Jacob noticed that Laban began to treat him differently. Sometime before that (even before Jacob's prosperity) the LORD God spoke to Jacob and told him to prepare to make this move (Gen. 31:1-13). Jacob told his wives about his grievance with their father and about the dream he had received from God with deliberate instructions for acquiring what would become his newfound wealth. He told them of God's command that Jacob must now return to Canaan. Both Rachel and Leah agreed with him without reservation.

Rachel and Leah speak about the "bride price" or "bridal dowry" – a gift the groom paid to his father-in-law. The text may suggest that it (the price of the gift) was meant to go to the bride herself as she entered her new husband's house. Laban, they both complained, had used the bride price (presumably Jacob's labor wages for him) without any concern for them, in effect disowning them. "His daughters thus see themselves reduced to chattel by their father, not married off but rather sold for profit, as though they were not his flesh and blood."[12] For this reason, they were now favoring their husband over their father. It's been said that people should "use money and love people." Laban, we might say, consistently acted in just the opposite manner. He "loved money and used people." His

---

12 Alter, Genesis: Translation and Commentary, 168.

daughters' justified disloyalty exemplifies the truth of another folk proverb: "The stingy man pays twice." Through the process of defrauding and using Jacob, Laban himself ended up losing valuable possessions. Everything was now set for Jacob's escape, this time away from Haran and back to his father's house.

Jacob's exodus from the land of servitude, which had once been a land of salvation, resonates with the story of Israel's exodus from Egypt. The children of Israel went to Egypt (in the time of Joseph) to escape a severe famine that was in the land, but in time became slaves of a new Pharaoh who was unwilling to let them go. Just as Jacob experienced God's intervention through dreams, so too did Joseph. Just as Jacob "breaks away" from a land of bondage with great wealth, Israel too, will leave Egypt with great wealth as a reparation payment for their forced slave labor. Another strong connection with the Exodus story is found in Genesis 46:3-4 where God says to Israel (Jacob): "Do not be afraid to go down to Egypt, for I will make you into a great nation there. I will go down to Egypt with you and I will surely bring you back again." This is similar to the words God spoke to Jacob at Bethel (Gen. 28:15). While there are differences between these stories, the similarities are stunning and clearly show authorial intent to draw such connections and parallels.

Jacob's exodus is back to the "land of your [i.e., his] birth" אֶל אֶרֶץ מוֹלַדְתֶּךָ (el erets moladtekha) in Gen. 31:13 while Abram's exodus from the same place was described as going "from the land of his birth" מֵאַרְצְךָ מוֹלַדְתֶּךָ (me-artsekha moladtekha). This indicates further evidence for the deliberately and artistically paralleled lives of these two men. Both journeys originate in Haran (11:31, 27:43, 28:10, 29:4), where they marry close relatives and leave fathers (Laban, Terah) and siblings (Abram's brothers and Laban's sons). They will follow the same itinerary through the land upon arriving and separating from other close relatives (Lot and Esau) because the land could not sustain their flocks (Gen. 13:6; 36:7). Genesis 31:20 speaks of Jacob literally "stealing the heart of Laban the Aramean":

41

וַיִּגְנֹב יַעֲקֹב אֶת־לֵב לָבָן הָאֲרַמִּי עַל־בְּלִי הִגִּיד לוֹ כִּי בֹרֵחַ הוּא

*Jacob kept Laban the Aramean in the dark, not telling him that he was fleeing.*
*(Gen. 31:20)*

The verb גָּנַב *(ganav)* "to steal" has a wide range of meanings in Hebrew (as in English). We may infer that not all actions described by this verb necessarily constitute morally negative acts. Here the phrase means to do something "quietly concealing," "without notice" or "in secret." We should note that Rachel in the previous verse 19 had also "stolen" תִּגְנֹב *(tignov)* idols from Laban, her father, so the story seems to be playing on the different meanings of the word. There may be other word plays here too. "Laban" לָבָן *(Lavan)*, whose name means "white," shares some sounds with the Hebrew word for "heart" לֵב *(lev)*, while the Hebrew word for "Aramean" אֲרַמִּי *(Arami)* sounds a bit like a Hebrew word for "deceiving" רָמָה *(ramah)*. What a fitting play on words, because when one thinks of Laban, one thinks of deception.[13]

Laban is called an "Aramean" in Gen 31, as if on purpose. "The stage is being set for the representation of the encounter between Laban (the Aramean) and Jacob (the Hebrew) as a negotiation between national entities."[14] Later on in the story, when Laban and Jacob make a peace and borders pact, they will both name the same heap of stones in their appropriate languages – Laban will use Aramaic and Jacob Hebrew (both meaning one and the same thing – "the heap of witness") – but for now we must not get too far ahead in the narrative.

When Jacob escaped, Laban was shearing his flock and was caught unaware. "Laban had earlier set a precedent of grazing his herds at a distance of three days' journey from Jacob's herds.... Other references to shearing of the flocks in the Bible indicate it was a very

---

13    Adele Berlin, and Marc Zvi Brettler, *The Jewish Study Bible: Torah, Nevi'im, Kethuvim*, 2nd ed. (New York: Oxford University Press, 2014), 59.
14    Alter, *Genesis: Translation and Commentary*, 169.

elaborate procedure involving large numbers of men, and accompanied by feasting, and so would have provided an excellent cover for Jacob's flight."[15]

Laban found out about it three days later, while his relatives were still with him. Laban pursued Jacob for seven days before catching up with him in the hill country of Gilead (Gen. 31:19-25). Some time prior to their meeting, God had appeared to Laban and warned him not to say anything to Jacob, either good or bad. In fact, both Abimelech and Laban received similar warnings regarding any mistreatment of Abram and Jacob (Gen. 20:3; 31:29). The one thing that Laban cannot understand is this: Why would Jacob (given his commitment to Abraham's God) steal his household gods/idols? Neither Jacob nor Laban imagined that Rachel was responsible for this. Jacob's rash statement, that anyone found with Laban's gods would be put to death, may have been a harbinger of Rachel's premature death at the birth of Benjamin (Gen. 35:16-20). It is not at all clear why she did what she did. As the narrative continues, the reason she remains undiscovered is because she remained seated upon the camel's packsaddle where the idols were hidden, offering the excuse that she was going through her menstrual period.

This may have been a personal revenge towards her father. Taking something that was very dear to him, in return for him having taken something important from her (both Jacob during the wedding, and her bridal dowry). On the other hand, "There is no reason to assume that Rachel would have become a strict monotheist through her marriage."[16] Like many people of that time she may have come to hold a henotheistic view (only one God is supreme and should be worshiped, but other gods also exist). A more positive reading of Rachel is proposed by Rashi – one of the key Jewish medieval Bible commentators. Rashi thinks that her intention was a noble one. Namely, to keep her father from the worship of idols.

---

[15]  Ibid.
[16]  Alter, *Genesis: Translation and Commentary*, 169.

Later, we will find that some Israelites when they left Egypt did not let go of the Egyptian idols, but took them on their journey. As late as the Israelite conquest of Canaan, Joshua had to issue his call to make a final break with the idols of Egypt: "If it is disagreeable in your sight to serve the LORD, choose for yourselves today whom you will serve: whether the gods which your fathers served which were beyond the River, or the gods of the Amorites in whose land you are living; but as for me and my house, we will serve the LORD" (Josh. 24:15).

Despite its seriousness, this story also contains a lot of humor and irony, especially if we pay attention to its literary style. There are many instances. One example is how Laban's paganism is ridiculed. His gods are protected and sat on by a menstruating woman. Lev. 15:22 will later state that everything upon which a menstruating woman sits is ceremonially unclean. In their direct speech, Laban (vs. 30) and Jacob (vs. 32) both refer to these stolen figurines as his "gods." But the story's narrator (vs. 34) describes them as idols or graven images תְּרָפִים *(terafim)*.[17]

Now Jacob speaks boldly to Laban, telling him what he always wanted to say to him face-to-face. He brings up all the unfaithfulness and trickery, and highlights his own endurance in the hardships of his service. Jacob describes his personal faithfulness to Laban over twenty long years.

Jacob also credits his current prosperity to the faithfulness of his God. We read in Genesis 31:42:

לוּלֵי אֱלֹהֵי אָבִי אֱלֹהֵי אַבְרָהָם וּפַחַד יִצְחָק הָיָה לִי כִּי עַתָּה רֵיקָם שִׁלַּחְתָּנִי אֶת־עָנְיִי וְאֶת־יְגִיעַ כַּפַּי רָאָה אֱלֹהִים וַיּוֹכַח אָמֶשׁ

17    Adele Berlin, and Marc Zvi Brettler, *The Jewish Study Bible: Torah, Neviim, Kethuvim*, 2nd ed (New York: Oxford University Press, 2014), 171.

*Had not the God of my father, the God of Abraham and the Fear of Isaac, been with me, you would have sent me away empty-handed. But God took notice of my plight and the toil of my hands, and He gave judgment last night. (Gen. 31:42)*

As we read this interaction, we cannot help but see Jacob as a man of integrity in his service of Laban; a man with a clear conscience as he boldly faces his uncle and publicly argues his case with the conviction of a righteous man. This may be the idea behind a later statement by the prophet Micah תִּתֵּן אֱמֶת לְיַעֲקֹב *(titen emet le-Yaakov)* "you (the LORD) gave truth to Jacob" (Mic. 7:20). Laban and Jacob agree to make a pact. This happens possibly because of the pressure of other relatives who listened as Laban was not able to establish any wrongdoing on the part of Jacob. Jacob agrees to treat his wives (Laban's daughters) well and commits not to take any additional wives. Laban's part was to leave Jacob alone and in peace.

The pact was made and was marked, characteristically, by the erection of a stone monument, followed by an oath exchange and communal meal to seal their agreement. Jacob's response to Laban's vows is set forth in Genesis 31:53:

אֱלֹהֵי אַבְרָהָם וֵאלֹהֵי נָחוֹר יִשְׁפְּטוּ בֵינֵינוּ אֱלֹהֵי אֲבִיהֶם וַיִּשָּׁבַע יַעֲקֹב בְּפַחַד אָבִיו יִצְחָק

*'May the God of Abraham and the god of Nahor" (their respective ancestral deities) "judge between us" and Jacob swore by the fear of his father Isaac. (Gen. 31:53)*

"Although it is not stated that Nahor emigrated with his father and brother from Ur of the Chaldees, Haran is called 'the city of Nahor' (Gen. 24:10), so it may be inferred that Nahor took part in the emigration and settled at Haran. Nahor was the progenitor of twelve Aramean tribes through his twelve sons, of whom eight were born to him by his wife Milcah, and four by his concubine Reumah (Gen. 22:20-24)."[18]

Alter writes, "Jacob swore by the Terror of his father Isaac. ...Jacob resists the universal Semitic term for God, *'elohim*, and the equation between the gods of Nahor and Abraham. He himself does not presume to go back as far as Abraham, but in the God of his father Isaac he senses something numinous, awesome, frightening."[19]

While in most English translations יִשְׁפְּטוּ בֵינֵינוּ *(yishfetu benenu)* is translated as "(God) judge between us," implying a single subject, the Hebrew actually uses a plural verb. The original thus clearly implies that it is not just one God, but two – the God of Abraham and the God of Nahor – who will give judgment jointly. It is easy to understand why people who live in a multi-god society would say something like this.

Jacob's confidence in fleeing Laban and his public confrontation with clear and fair charges were all based on his imperfect, yet real, confidence in the promises of God. God promised to keep Jacob safe and, in spite of all his deserved and undeserved troubles, to have him become the father of a great nation with its own land, protected and blessed by Abraham's God.

## The Danger of Return

Over twenty years have passed since Jacob ran away from his brother destitute and alone. More than twenty years have passed since Esau swore his revenge for the theft of his blessing. Now the brothers are about to meet again. In the past Esau had sworn to kill Jacob. Will he do so now? Or could it be that time (and the God of Abraham, Isaac and Jacob) had softened his heart? Now, in the final stage of

---

[18] Emil G. Hirsch and Seligsohn, M. (1906), "Nahor." *Jewish Encyclopedia*, accessed December 19, 2015, http://www.jewishencyclopedia.com/articles/11287-nahor

[19] Alter, *Genesis: Translation and Commentary*, 176.

Jacob's struggle with his brother, he must come face-to-face with him once again. God's covenant promise is God's gift for the future. But God endowed Jacob with entrepreneurial ingenuity, a gift he used all the time. I realize that I have just stated something here that goes completely against the usual interpretation. The traditional Christian interpretation proposes that all Jacob's "survival plans" were an expression of his doubt.

There is a notion that only after meeting with God at Penuel did Jacob gain trust towards God and, because of that, was renamed Israel. I clearly don't think that this is a good reconstruction of the events. Jacob's faith does not have to be in conflict with Jacob's shrewd preparations. As we will see later, Jacob is not simply bribing his way back to peace. Something far more important is happening in the story. When Laban and his company left, Jacob continued on his way to Canaan. In Genesis 32:2 we read about an unexplained and unannounced encounter with the "angels of God" מַלְאֲכֵי אֱלֹהִים (malakhe Elohim). After this brief mention we are told that Jacob declared, "This is God's camp" and named the place מַחֲנָיִם (machanayim). This word translated literally means "the two camps" or "a pair of camps."

Jacob understood that he had just encountered God's angels carrying out His will (i.e. protecting him) while he was heading to Canaan, just as he saw them at Bethel on the way out of Canaan many years earlier. "There is a marked narrative symmetry between Jacob's departure from Canaan, when he had his dream of angels at Bethel, and his return, when again he encounters a company of angels. That symmetry will be unsettled when later in the chapter he finds himself in fateful conflict with a single divine being."[20]

Jacob divided everything into two camps. His plan was simple. If things don't work out as he hopes, at least one of his camps will remain alive and survive the meeting with Esau and his 400 warriors.

---

[20]    Alter, *Genesis: Translation and Commentary*, 176.

Perhaps, Jacob reasoned that this is what God had in mind. This sounds remarkably similar to Abraham and Sarah's struggle with child-conception, and their creative "Hagar solution" to help God to keep His word (Gen. 16:1). But while we have the privilege of knowing how things turned out, Jacob did not. We know that no planning was needed, that Esau was coming to meet his brother in peace. But Jacob did not know this. He acted responsibly in having a "plan B."

## Public Repentance

We read in Genesis 32:4-6 that Jacob, upon his approach to Seir, the country of Edom where Esau now lived, sends his messengers ahead of him as part of his elaborate plan:

וַיְצַו אֹתָם לֵאמֹר כֹּה תֹאמְרוּן לַאדֹנִי לְעֵשָׂו כֹּה אָמַר עַבְדְּךָ יַעֲקֹב עִם־לָבָן גַּרְתִּי וָאֵחַר עַד־עָתָּה

*"And instructed them as follows, thus shall you say, 'To my lord Esau, thus says your servant Jacob: I stayed with Laban and remained until now'." (Gen. 32:4/5)*

Jacob is between a rock and a hard place, i.e., Laban and Esau! He cannot return to Laban because of the agreement with him, and he cannot yet return home – he must meet Esau first. He continues:

וַיְהִי־לִי שׁוֹר וַחֲמוֹר צֹאן וְעֶבֶד וְשִׁפְחָה וָאֶשְׁלְחָה לְהַגִּיד לַאדֹנִי לִמְצֹא־חֵן בְּעֵינֶיךָ

*"I have acquired cattle, asses, sheep, and male and female slaves; and I send this message to my lord in the hope of gaining your favor." (Gen. 32:5/6)*

There is one central issue of note here. The messengers (in this case human, not angelic servants) are instructed to refer to their master as עַבְדְּךָ יַעֲקֹב (avdekha Yaakov) "your servant Jacob" when speaking to Esau, while referring to Esau as Jacob's lord, לַאדֹנִי לְעֵשָׂו (l-adoni le-Esav) "to my lord Esau." This idea is repeated as Jacob approaches

48

Esau in the hope of reconciliation. Jacob no longer wants the blessing of dominance over his brother that he stole. By these repeated symbolic actions, Jacob strives to communicate clearly that both the right and the blessings of the firstborn do indeed belong to Esau and not to him. Jacob is now a great man who is both blessed by God with the blessing of Abraham and repentant in every way toward the brother he wronged many years ago. The plan is not simply some manipulation to get what he wants and to secure a safe passage home. The central part of the plan is a ceremony of public repentance and reparation of the wrongs done. Jacob knows from his struggles with Leah, Rachel, and Laban (and of course with himself) that love (even brotherly love) is not sufficient.

Jacob has learned, over time and through many struggles, to listen both to God and to the cries of those around him. As he struggled with the insecurities of both Leah and Rachel, Jacob became a different man. He would no longer "walk over corpses" to get what he needed. He now understands the deep human need for justice and righteousness. He has learned that love without justice is not sufficient. Those less-loved must be treated with honor and dignity; with sensitivity and care. Jacob has learned what Israel will later be commanded to learn – to listen (*Shema*). According to Rabbi Sacks, in Jewish tradition

> the highest spiritual gift is the ability to listen – not only to the voice of God, but also to the cry of other people, the sigh of the poor, the weak, the lonely, the neglected and, yes, sometimes the un-loved or less-loved. That is one of the meanings of the great command: *Shema Yisrael*, "Listen, O Israel." Jacob's other name, we recall, was Israel… He is the most tenacious of all the patriarchs and the only one whose children all become part of the covenant. It is rather that every virtue has a corresponding danger. Those who are courageous are often unaware of the fears of ordinary people. Those of penetrating intellect are often dismissive of lesser minds. Those who, like Jacob, have an unusual capacity to love must fight against the danger of failing to honor the feelings of those they do not love with equal passion. The antidote is the ability to listen. That is what Jacob discovered in the course of his life, and why he, above all, is

the role model for the Jewish people the nation commanded to listen.[21]

But there is something else of great importance in Jacob's response to the messenger's news. We read in Genesis 32:7/8:

וַיִּירָא יַעֲקֹב מְאֹד וַיֵּצֶר לוֹ

*Jacob was greatly afraid and distressed. (Gen. 32:7/8)*

Normally we understand this as Jacob being afraid for his life and the lives of his loved ones. However, this may have not been the case, given the repetitive wording. Jewish sages have speculated that Jacob was not only afraid that he would be killed, but that he would kill also. Remember the fear of Rebekah, Jacob, and Esau's mother, that if they were to meet they might kill each other! (Gen. 27:45) Israelite theology sees any human killing as problematic and Jewish theologians spend massive amounts of time thinking about the ethical implications of all imaginable life situations. Even when there is clarity about a situation, such as a thief who is killed during a night intrusion (Ex.22:2-3), the killing of the thief is a justified but still regrettable thing. "In a conflict between two rights or two wrongs, there may be a proper way to act – the lesser of two evils, or the greater of two goods – but this does not cancel out all emotional pain."[22] We read in an early Midrash about the following discussion:

> "Rabbi Judah bar Ilai said: Are not fear and distress identical? The meaning, however, is that "he was afraid" that he might be killed; "he was distressed" that he might kill. For Jacob thought: If he prevails against me, will he not kill me; while if I prevail against him, will I not kill him? That is the meaning of "he was afraid" – lest he should be killed; "and distressed" – lest he should kill." (Bereshit Rabbah 76:2).

---

21  Sacks, *Covenant & Conversation*, 209.
22  *Ibid.*, 217.

Only people who know how to experience, "not only the physical fear of defeat but the moral distress of victory… and are capable of feeling both, can defend their bodies without endangering their souls."[23]

## Jacob's Prayer

The messengers returned to Jacob with disturbing news. Esau himself, in the company of four hundred men, was now approaching. Jacob was truly afraid, and he had every good reason. After following through with his plan to divide his household into two camps, he did what all great men of faith do when met with an enormous challenge, he prayed humbly, but boldly.

> Oh God of my father Abraham and God of my father Isaac, O LORD, who said to me, "Return to your native land and I will deal bountifully with you"! I am unworthy of all the kindness that You have so steadfastly shown Your servant: with my staff alone I crossed this Jordan, and now I have become two camps. Deliver me, I pray, from the hand of my brother, from the hand of Esau; else, I fear, he may come and strike me down, mothers and children alike. Yet You have said, "I will deal bountifully with you and make your offspring as the sands of the sea, which are too numerous to count." (Gen. 32:10/11-12/13)

First, Jacob appeals to the LORD God based upon his connection to his fathers – Abraham and Isaac. Second, he appeals to God's direct command to leave Haran and return home. Third, he confesses that he is unworthy of any goodness that the LORD has demonstrated to him so far. Fourth, he asks for God's deliverance from the hand of Esau, being afraid also for the lives of all those with him. And fifth, Jacob holds the LORD God to his own promise that he will be treated well by Him and that his descendants would become abundantly numerous. If Jacob and his family do not survive this day, clearly God's words cannot be trusted. Jacob, ending with a recital of God's promise and holding God up to this promise, shows

---

[23]   *Ibid.*, 218.

that, in the end, he did not count on his own smart "kissing-up-to-Esau" plan. In the end he trusted in God, who has kept His word and whose promises one can truly rely upon. In this, his faith resembled that of his grandfather Abraham. A faith like this is best seen in the story of the "binding of Isaac." There, as well, God's promises and the God-arranged events in Abraham's life seemed to be at odds with each other. Jacob not only had the blessing of Abraham, he now also had the faith of Abraham and his ability to trust God.

## Restitution and Confession

After a sleepless night, Jacob organized the reconciliation gifts intended for his older brother. In Genesis 32:14/15-15/16 we are given an exact description of his gifts: "200 she-goats and 20 he-goats; 200 ewes and 20 rams; 30 milch (milk) camels with their colts; 40 cows and 10 bulls; 20 she-asses and 10 he-asses." The proportions of male and female animals here are not coincidental. Jacob sought to communicate that with this balance Esau is set for exponential growth of his livestock. When the number of males and females is about the same, the growth would be a lot slower, but when the percentage of males and females is such as we see here, prolific increase is almost guaranteed.

Walking separated from each other in groups, Jacob's plan was to gradually soften the heart of his brother Esau and thus receive his forgiveness. Each group was to give Esau exactly the same message: "Your servant Jacob's gift sent to my lord Esau... and he (Jacob) himself is right behind us." (Gen. 32:18/19) We read in Genesis 32:20/21:

וַאֲמַרְתֶּם גַּם הִנֵּה עַבְדְּךָ יַעֲקֹב אַחֲרֵינוּ כִּי־אָמַר אֲכַפְּרָה פָנָיו בַּמִּנְחָה הַהֹלֶכֶת לְפָנָי
וְאַחֲרֵי־כֵן אֶרְאֶה פָנָיו אוּלַי יִשָּׂא פָנָי

*And you shall add, 'And your servant Jacob himself is right behind us.'" For he reasoned, "If I propitiate him with presents in advance, and then face him, perhaps he will show me favor." (Gen. 32:20/21)*

The Hebrew word פָּנִים (*panim*), which literally means "face," occurs seven times in this passage (Gen. 32:17-21). If we don't regard that fact as coincidental, it might indicate the idea of completion. This (especially vs. 21) builds a case and connects with the place being called פְּנִיאֵל (*Penuel*), which means "face of God" (Gen. 32:31/32). This all underscores the association of Esau with the mysterious figure with whom Jacob is about to wrestle. This same concept of "face-to-face" encounters is used in the case of Moses (Ex. 33:11, Deut. 34:10) and Gideon (Jud. 6:22). As the gifts slowly make their way to Esau, Jacob remains in the camp, giving enough time for his reconciliation offerings to be received. That night, taking his family, "he crossed the ford" of the Jabbok וַיַּעֲבֹר אֵת מַעֲבַר (*va-yaavor et maavar*). The word for "ford" here is מַעֲבַר (*maavar*). It is connected with the verb עָבַר (*avar*) "to cross over." The Jabbok is an offshoot spring of the Jordan River, running from East to West. Jacob has been traveling south from the high country of Gilead. Esau is heading north from Edom to meet him. Once Jacob's family reached the other side, he sent over all his remaining possessions. Jacob, however, stayed behind.

The text says that he was now left alone. His next surprise encounter will confirm all that was already true of Jacob. Jacob is all about struggle. "Both his names – *Jacob*, 'he who grasps by the heel,' and *Israel*, 'he who struggles with G-d and man and prevails' – convey a sense of conflict... The gifts he has, he has fought for. None have come naturally. Jacob is the supreme figure of persistence."[24] The name change to Israel resembles that given to Sarai – Sarah (Gen. 17:15), since both involve the same root שָׂר (*sar*). The association of Sarah's new name with royalty is explicitly made in Gen. 17:16.

---

[24] Jonathan Sacks, *Covenant & Conversation*, http://rabbisacks.org/covenant-conversation-5768-vayetse-leahs-tears/

Jacob's name will be changed to reflect the obvious reality in his life – he was a man born to overcome.

## Two Meetings

In Genesis 32:24-25 we are told that when Jacob sent his family over the river he was left alone. He had done all he could – he sent reconciliatory gifts, he prayed to the LORD, he even prepared his household for a military confrontation. Now he was alone. And this is what took place that night in Genesis 32:25-26:

וַיִּוָּתֵר יַעֲקֹב לְבַדּוֹ וַיֵּאָבֵק אִישׁ עִמּוֹ עַד עֲלוֹת הַשָּׁחַר

*Jacob was left alone. And a man wrestled with him until the break of dawn. (Gen. 32:24/25)*

וַיַּרְא כִּי לֹא יָכֹל לוֹ וַיִּגַּע בְּכַף־יְרֵכוֹ וַתֵּקַע כַּף־יֶרֶךְ יַעֲקֹב בְּהֵאָבְקוֹ עִמּוֹ

*When he saw that he had not prevailed against him, he wrenched Jacob's hip at its socket, so that the socket of his hip was strained as he wrestled with him. (Gen. 32:25/26)*

This root אָבַק *(avak)* "to wrestle" is found only here in these two Bible verses and apparently plays on the similar-sounding names of the river Jabbok יַבֹּק *(Yavok)* and of Jacob himself יַעֲקֹב *(Yaakov)*. The geographical locale and the events that take place there are punned together. So the river becomes associated with "the place of the supplanter's struggle." It is not clear from the text who it was that wrestled with Jacob, nor why. What is clear is that Jacob himself did not expect this meeting and this fight. His mind was naturally preoccupied with meeting Esau. The text states that it was אִישׁ *(ish)* "a man" that wrestled with Jacob. Later, the prophet Hosea depicts him as "angel/messenger of God" (Hosea 12:4). Some Rabbinic sages thought it was Esau's guardian angel who came to oppose him, while others thought it was Satan himself. In the end, Jacob was convinced beyond a shadow of a doubt that he had wrestled with

God. "And he took leave of him there. So Jacob named the place Penuel, meaning, "I have seen a divine being face to face, yet my life has been preserved" (Gen. 32:31).

## Why Now?

A truly intriguing and original interpretation was suggested by an 11th-century Jewish commentator, Rashbam. He suggested that this event must be connected with other events in which great people, called by God to something important, suddenly doubted their mission and, perhaps, were tempted to reconsider the validity of God's call and in some way to disobey it. A truly puzzling, but very important event in the life of Moses when the LORD Himself (similar to this meeting with Jacob) came to Moses and sought his death, must be mentioned. Only the quick action of Zipporah in circumcising their son saved Moses from sure death (Ex. 4:24-25). Joshua, before confronting Jericho's tall walls was also met by "a man," who turned out to be the Commander of the LORD's armies, his sword already drawn.

What was curious about Joshua's meeting is that, just as with Jacob, "the man" also seemed to be God Himself. Joshua "fell on his face to the earth and worshiped him," and was commanded to take off his shoes because of the holiness of the ground upon which he stood (Josh. 5:13-15). This particular encounter parallels exactly the one between Moses and God at the burning bush. Both removed their shoes because of the holiness of the place (Ex. 3:5). "The confrontation" is one of the common factors in each encounter. As a result, God's struggle with His own chosen people appears to be a major theme. We can recall other times when God just would not let something happen. For example, Jonah tried to evade the Nineveh mission, but God pursued him and compelled him to accomplish the task. Balaam, on the way to cursing Israel was literally stopped by the Angel of the LORD (Num. 22:21-35). The examples are numerous, and they seem to form a pattern. When something vitally important, in a covenantal sense, is imminent, God intervenes to ensure it happens.

## A New Name

The man who fought with Jacob blessed him, and in blessing him he changed his name to Israel. We read about it in Genesis 32:28-29:

וַיֹּאמֶר אֵלָיו מַה־שְּׁמֶךָ וַיֹּאמֶר יַעֲקֹב

*Said the other, "What is your name?" He replied, "Jacob." (Gen. 32:27/28)*

וַיֹּאמֶר לֹא יַעֲקֹב יֵאָמֵר עוֹד שִׁמְךָ כִּי אִם־יִשְׂרָאֵל כִּי־שָׂרִיתָ עִם־אֱלֹהִים וְעִם־אֲנָשִׁים וַתּוּכָל

*Said he, "Your name shall no longer be Jacob, but Israel, for you have striven with beings divine and human, and have prevailed." (Gen. 32:28/29)*

Names in the ancient Jewish world were far more important than they are for many today. In the biblical culture they carried a very important weight. A name spoke of a person's character, his deeds and his identity. For a person to be given a new name, meant a change in their identity. That Jacob's name was "Jacob" (the heel-grabber) was, of course, known to the one who attacked him. This divine being (whoever he may have been) probably asked Jacob's name as a part of the name-changing process. But before he could assign Jacob a new name, Jacob himself had understood the name he was now leaving behind. After this "heel-grabbing" acknowledgement Jacob's name changed to Israel. The word "Israel" most likely comes from the root שָׂר *(sar)*, which in biblical Hebrew means "to struggle" and "to exercise influence," "to rule as a prince."

Jacob became Israel precisely because he struggled with and overcame both Heaven and Earth, both God and humanity. There is "some question about its meaning, though an educated guess about the original sense of the name would be: 'God will rule,' or perhaps, 'God will prevail.'"[25] Another important observation should also be mentioned. While this אִישׁ *(ish)* "man" changes Jacob's name to Israel, in Genesis 35:9-10 it is clear that God does so. It is worth noting that Genesis 32:31/32 states that: "The sun rose upon him as he passed Penuel, limping because of his hip." We might recall that in Genesis 28:11 we read "And he came to a certain place and stayed there that night, because the sun had set." The sun "setting" at the beginning of Jacob's journey and in its end, seems to bracket the transformation journey of Jacob becoming Israel. God appears to Jacob when he reaches home and blesses him there, telling him that from then on, his name will no longer be Jacob, but Israel.[26] God identifies himself as *El Shaddai* and confirms the blessing of Abraham upon him (Gen. 35:11-13).

**Father of the Nation Israel**

It is only much later, after the fall of the Northern Kingdom of Israel that the people of Israel as a whole would begin to be called "Judeans" or "Jews." This is not a biblical injunction, but merely a historical reality identifying survivors with the Southern Kingdom of Judah and its lands. In biblical terms, the true name of the covenantal descendants of Abraham, Isaac and Jacob is not "Jews," but "Israelites" – the children of the man whose name was changed by this very encounter with the divine. The modern term "Jews" came to be because those who returned from Babylon lived in Judea and so all (regardless of original tribe) were called "Judeans." Over time even those living in diaspora were identified with Judea and called "Jews."

But why did this unexpected meeting happen right before the meeting with Esau? The basic answer in my view is that the founder

---

25    Alter, *Genesis: Translation and Commentary*, 182.
26    What is striking is that in contrast to Abram/Abraham, the Torah continues to use Jacob/Israel interchangeably.

of Israel as a nation could not have been a thief, a liar and a coward. We must remember that the Book of Genesis is a prelude to the Book of Exodus, which was written for Israelites who departed from Egypt and were on their way to Canaan. Jacob needed to become Israel. It took twenty-two years of exile to accomplish this. He had now changed and was ready. He possessed the blessing of Abraham (land and children), but he needed to return the blessing he had stolen which was not his own (power and wealth). This reconciliation with Esau was not simply a personal family affair, as it must surely have seemed to Jacob and Esau. It was an event of global significance, for the very identity of the future nation of Israel was at stake.

Their father, called by the same name as they, was in fact the rightful owner of the covenant blessing of Abraham and Isaac. When he learned the truth he acted upon it courageously, being willing to face Esau and return to him that which was rightly his. Once that was accomplished, everything that Jacob/Israel had would legitimately belong to him and his children. Israelites were not thieves and robbers, but the legitimate custodians of the divinely promised land. This is bigger than Jacob and Esau. If Rashbam is right, it was God, in the moment of Jacob's weakness, who was determined to stop Jacob from running away from this fundamentally important meeting. The stakes were too high for Jacob to fail. He was not simply Jacob, he was the founder of the nation of Israel – a people who would be blessed by the LORD God, and a people who existed in order to bless all others (Gen. 32:32-33; Gen. 12:1-3).

**Unexpected Grace**

After the encounter with the mysterious man, Jacob crossed the Jabbok, where his family was waiting for him. Jacob saw Esau and his delegation from afar. He told both wives and both concubines to stand with their children. The two concubines were to go first, followed by Leah and her children, and Rachel and her son Joseph followed last. (Gen.33:1-3). As Esau approached, Jacob went to the front of his family procession and bowed down seven times as he came closer. This tradition of bowing down or prostrating seven times is attested to in ancient documents as a sign of homage that a vassal king shows to his suzerain master (Tel El Amarna Letters). This scene reverses the dominance of Jacob over Esau prophesied in Genesis 25:23 and 27:29, 37.[27]

Much later, when the Israelites who left Egypt heard this story, they were probably shocked at how things developed. We read in Genesis 33:4:

וַיָּרָץ עֵשָׂו לִקְרָאתוֹ וַיְחַבְּקֵהוּ וַיִּפֹּל עַל־צַוָּארָו וַיִּשָּׁקֵהוּ וַיִּבְכּוּ

*Esau ran to greet him. He embraced him and, falling on his neck, he kissed him; and they wept. (Gen. 33:4)*

Perhaps Esau's rage and swearing to kill his brother was nothing more than a manifestation of his impulsive personality. The same personality which we saw displayed when he so carelessly sold his birthright for food. Esau was fully prepared to formally forgive his brother. When people are hesitant about their offer of forgiveness they don't run towards the one who offended them. Esau ran to Jacob. Esau had probably forgiven Jacob a long time ago, and now, at the opportunity of their meeting, Esau's healed emotions could be expressed to show how much he truly loved his younger brother after all. As the brothers continued to greet one another, Esau looked up and saw the women and children. He then asked about who they were, to which Jacob responded:

הַיְלָדִים אֲשֶׁר־חָנַן אֱלֹהִים אֶת־עַבְדֶּךָ

*"The children with whom God has favored your servant." (Gen. 33:5)*

---

[27] Jon D. Levenson, "Genesis Introductions and Annotations," in *The Jewish Study Bible. Tanakh Translation,* eds. Adele Berlin and Marc Zvi Brettler (New York: Oxford University Press, 2014), 63.

The emphasis here is upon God's grace in giving him many children, and also upon him being Esau's humble and submissive servant. Everything that Jacob says and does speaks of his servitude to his brother, not the other way around. It was not only Jacob himself, but also his wives and children, who were said to be Esau's servants as they too approached and bowed before Jacob's older brother (Gen. 33:6-7).

Esau then asked about the meaning of all the animal groups that he met one after another on the way to greet Jacob. Jacob responded that he sent those "to find grace in your eyes, my lord" לִמְצֹא־חֵן בְּעֵינֵי אֲדֹנִי *(limtso chen be-eyne adoni)*. This phraseology is still in use today. In Modern Hebrew, one way to ask someone if they liked something is to ask them literally if it "found grace in their eyes." [28] Esau's response is:

יֶשׁ־לִי רָב אָחִי יְהִי לְךָ אֲשֶׁר־לָךְ

*I have plenty, my brother. Let what you have remain yours. (Gen. 33:9)*

Jacob then said to Esau:

אַל־נָא אִם־נָא מָצָאתִי חֵן בְּעֵינֶיךָ וְלָקַחְתָּ מִנְחָתִי מִיָּדִי כִּי עַל־כֵּן רָאִיתִי פָנֶיךָ כִּרְאֹת פְּנֵי אֱלֹהִים וַתִּרְצֵנִי

*No, I pray you; if you would do me this favor, accept from me this gift; for to see your face is like seeing the face of God, and you have received me favorably. (Gen. 33:10)*

קַח־נָא אֶת־בִּרְכָתִי אֲשֶׁר הֻבָאת לָךְ כִּי־חַנַּנִי אֱלֹהִים וְכִי יֶשׁ־לִי־כֹל וַיִּפְצַר־בּוֹ וַיִּקָּח

*Please accept my present which has been brought to you, for God has favored me and I have plenty." And when he urged him, he accepted. (Gen. 33:11)*

---

[28]   This reconciliation between "Edom" and Jacob/Israel is perhaps another harbinger of the future when both will be part of the same inheritance (Amos 9:12, Obadiah 19-21). The name "Edom" is used explicitly in Gen. 32:4.

60

Jacob and Esau's assessment of what they own is not the same. This is a point most Bible translations miss. While Esau says יֶשׁ־לִי רָב (yesh li rav), which means "I have plenty," Jacob states יֶשׁ־לִי־כֹל (yesh li kol), which means "I have everything." One speaks of a large quantity, while the other speaks of sufficiency. The verb פָּצַר (patsar) in this Hebrew sentence implies a very forceful insistence by Jacob: Jacob "urged" his brother. A crucial point not to be overlooked in this passage is that Jacob has frequently been using the word מִנְחָה (minchah), commonly translated "gift," as he does in verse 10, but in verse 11 this suddenly changes. Instead of מִנְחָתִי (minchati) "my gift," Jacob asks Esau to take בִּרְכָתִי (birkhati) "my blessing." Jacob is not simply "kissing up" to Esau, he is "returning" the blessing he stole.

We would be remiss if we did not pay attention to verse 10 where Jacob explains that to see the forgiving and welcoming face of Esau was "like seeing the face of God" כִּרְאֹת פְּנֵי אֱלֹהִים (ki-reot pene Elohim). We have noted before how the idea of פָּנִים (panim), variously translated as "face" or "presence" (among other things), is certainly a common and possibly key word in the Jacob narratives. Of course this will not only be limited to Jacob, because the stories about the nation of Israel and her dealings with the God of Abraham, Isaac and Jacob will continue this same trajectory. Here, suffice it to say, Jacob himself clearly connected these two encounters. For him, the confrontation with "the man" of Penuel (meaning "the *face* of God") and the meeting with Esau, were clearly connected (vs. 10b). The various uses of פָּנִים (panim) in Hebrew abound in chapters 32-33, but most instances simply cannot be seen in our English translations. Rabbi Sacks writes:

> To take one example, Genesis 32: 21 is translated: [Jacob said to his servants,] "You shall say, 'Your servant Jacob is coming behind us,'" for he thought, "I will pacify him with these gifts I am sending on ahead; later, when I see him, perhaps he will receive me." There is nothing in the English translation to suggest that the word פָּנִים (panim) actually appears four times in this verse alone. But the second half of the verse could be literally translated: "for he

thought, 'I will wipe [the anger from] his face with the gift that goes ahead of my face; afterward, when I see his face perhaps he will lift up my face….'" There is a drama here and it has to do with faces: the face of Esau, of Jacob, and of God Himself.[29]

---

29   Sacks, *Covenant & Conversation*, 223.

# CHAPTER TWO: THE HIDDEN STORY JACOB'S CHILDREN

The "Joseph story" picks up in Genesis 37:1 with the statement that Jacob dwelled in the land of Canaan, the land where Abraham sojourned before him. This should not be glossed over. The story that the narrator is about to tell takes place at a particular point in time, a significant moment. Jacob firmly settled in the very land where Abraham was only a guest. Joseph assisted his older brothers (Dan, Naphtali, Gad and Asher) in shepherding the flock. One possible way to interpret the Hebrew text is as literally saying something like "he was being their young man" וְהוּא נַעַר אֶת־בְּנֵי בִלְהָה וְאֶת־בְּנֵי זִלְפָּה *(ve-hu naar et bene Vilhah ve-et bene Zilpah)*. In other words, he did the jobs of an errand boy that his older brothers did not want to do. (Gen. 37:2).

Most of the things that happen to Joseph give an impression of him being passive, i.e. things were usually done *to* him by someone else. This would only be true until his brothers' arrival to his residence in Egypt. Like Jacob his father, Joseph had character flaws. The text speaks of him bringing "evil reports" to his father regarding his brothers (Gen. 37:2). One may understand this in various senses. Joseph is perhaps accused of habitual tale-bearing on his brothers. But we may also understand that there were legitimate evils to be reported and dealt with. Joseph might have simply reported or carried what his brothers said to him. In the end, his brothers were guilty of wanting to kill him, so perhaps the reports were indeed justified.

וְיִשְׂרָאֵל אָהַב אֶת־יוֹסֵף מִכָּל־בָּנָיו כִּי־בֶן־זְקֻנִים הוּא לוֹ וְעָשָׂה לוֹ כְּתֹנֶת פַּסִּים:

*Now Israel loved Joseph more than all his sons because he was a son born to him late in life, and he made a special tunic for him. (Gen. 37:3)*

63

We are told that Israel loved Joseph more than his brothers because he was born to him in his old age. We cannot help but wonder why the narrator does not mention that Joseph was the son of Rachel, Jacob's special love. Be that as it may, *Israel* openly expressed his favoritism by giving Joseph a very special tunic. In Hebrew it is called כְּתֹנֶת פַּסִּים *(ketonet passim),* which clearly showed him to be loved above his brothers. The traditional idea seen in many English translations and folklore is that this was some sort of multi-colored outer garment. But the meaning of the Hebrew is not completely clear and there is no way to know for sure. Alter comments, "We are told that the *ketonet pasim* was worn by virgin princesses. It is thus a unisex garment and a product of ancient haute couture."[30]

This was most likely the kind of robe worn by royalty. In Genesis 37:8 his brothers asked him rhetorically if Joseph is going to be a king over them. We read in 37:4 that the older brothers became so filled with envy and hatred towards Joseph that they could not even say "shalom" to him וְלֹא יָכְלוּ דַּבְּרוֹ לְשָׁלֹם *(ve-lo yakhlu dabro le-shalom).* But how do they move from truly disliking Joseph to harboring resentment which leads to his kidnapping and attempted murder?

**The Fateful Dreams**

What seemed to push the brothers over the line (although of course their murderous violence towards Joseph was inexcusable) is that he began to dream dreams. In one dream that he relates to his brothers, he saw himself as an upright sheaf while the sheaves of his brothers were bowing before him (Gen. 37:5-8). In another dream, which Joseph naively relayed to his brothers and his father, he saw the moon and the sun, along with eleven stars bowing before him. His father rebuked him. But, while his brothers' jealousy grew only more intense, Jacob kept this matter in his thoughts, wondering exactly what it might mean given the clear interpretation of the second dream (Gen. 37:9-11).

---

30  Alter, *Genesis: Translation and Commentary,* 209.

It is interesting to note that the brothers were so obsessed with disdain towards Joseph that they ignored the meaning of the dreams entirely. They dismissed the prophetic nature and focused only on the suggestions of subservience to their younger brother. Moreover, "as has often been noted, the dreams in the Joseph story reflect its more secular orientation in comparison with the preceding narratives in Genesis. They are not direct messages from God, like His appearance in the dream-visions to Abimelech and to Jacob."[31] Joseph's account of his dreams shows a young man who is self-absorbed, naively assuming that all involved will be equally fascinated by the content of his dreams. The text repeats the Hebrew word הִנֵּה (hineh) "behold" three times in the space of only one verse, perhaps highlighting Joseph's fascination with the dream (Gen. 37:7; then twice in vs. 9). Alter notes further:

> It should also be observed that doublets are a recurrent principle of organization in the Joseph story, just as binary divisions are an organizing principle in the Jacob story. Joseph and Pharaoh have double dreams; the chief butler and the chief baker dream their pair of seemingly parallel, actually antithetical dreams. Joseph is first flung into a pit and later into the prison-house. The brothers make two trips down to Egypt, with one of their number seemingly at risk on each occasion. And their descent to Egypt with goods and silver mirrors the descent of the merchant caravan, bearing the same items that first brought Joseph down to Egypt.[32]

## The Plot to Kill

It is not clear what Israel was thinking when he sent a 17-year-old Joseph, too well-dressed for what seems to be a job, on a fairly long errand from Hebron all the way to Shechem where his brothers were tending the livestock. When Joseph arrived near Shechem, he found out that his brothers had gone even further away to Dothan. When his brothers saw him from afar, they immediately began to conspire

---

[31]  *Ibid.*, 209.
[32]  *Ibid.*, 210.

how to get rid of him once and for all. Even their opening words are chilling, anticipating the violence that is to follow. In English Joseph is often labeled simply as a "dreamer," but the Hebrew term בַּעַל הַחֲלֹמוֹת (*baal ha-chalomot*) is stronger and, in the Hebrew context, likely more sarcastic. The term בַּעַל (*baal*) "master" suggests someone who has a special "proprietary relation to, or mastery of, the noun that follows it."[33] This means that the brothers (probably mockingly) described Joseph as a "master of dreams."

Ancient texts are often hard to read. This terminology could be showing that in the minds of the brothers, Joseph's dreams were something he himself is responsible for – that they are of his own doing. Or, it could be pointing out that he simply had an abundance of colorful dreams. Again, the hate-filled, conspiring brothers completely miss the point of Joseph's dreaming. It has been said, "When you are holding a hammer, everything begins to look like a nail."

Speculatively, perhaps Joseph's brothers even went further from home with the flocks in the expectation that he would come and could be lured further away from home (though we don't know that for sure). Maybe they were already lying in wait for Joseph.

Of course, not all the brothers were a part of the plot to kill him. We learn that Joseph had "the bad judgment to wear on his errand the garment that was the extravagant token of his father's favoritism."[34]

וְעַתָּה לְכוּ וְנַהַרְגֵהוּ וְנַשְׁלִכֵהוּ בְּאַחַד הַבֹּרוֹת וְאָמַרְנוּ חַיָּה רָעָה אֲכָלָתְהוּ וְנִרְאֶה מַה־יִּהְיוּ

*Come now, let's kill him, throw him into one of the cisterns, and then say that a wild animal ate him. Then we'll see how his dreams turn out! (Gen. 37:20)*

---

33   *Ibid.*, 212.
34   *Ibid.*, 213.

וַיְהִי כַּאֲשֶׁר־בָּא יוֹסֵף אֶל־אֶחָיו וַיַּפְשִׁיטוּ אֶת־יוֹסֵף אֶת־כֻּתָּנְתּוֹ אֶת־כְּתֹנֶת הַפַּסִּים
אֲשֶׁר עָלָיו: וַיִּקָּחֻהוּ וַיַּשְׁלִכוּ אֹתוֹ הַבֹּרָה

*When Joseph reached his brothers, they stripped him of his tunic, the special tunic that he wore. Then they took him and threw him into the cistern. (Gen. 37:23–24)*

We read in Genesis 27:22 that Reuben tried to save Joseph by tricking the brothers. "Reuben tries not to contradict the violence of his brothers' feelings toward Joseph and uses the same phrase, to fling him[35] into a pit, with the crucial difference that in his proposal it is a live Joseph who will be cast into the pit."[36] Sacks comments as follows:

> It is a confusing episode. Who pulled Joseph from the pit? Who sold him to the Ishmaelites? Was it the brothers or the Midianites? The subject, "they," is ambiguous. Commentators offer many interpretations. Of these, the simplest is given by Rashbam, who reads it as follows: The brothers, having thrown Joseph into the pit, sat down some distance away to eat. Reuben sneaked back to rescue Joseph, but found the pit empty and cried, "The boy is not! And I, where can I go? Rashbam points out that the brothers did not calm him down by telling him that they had sold Joseph. They seem as surprised as he was. It follows that the brothers, having seen the Ishmaelites in the distance, decided to sell Joseph to them, but before they had the chance to do so, a second group of travelers, the Midianites, heard Joseph's cries, saw the possibility of selling him to the Ishmaelites, and did so.[37]

There is also a simpler explanation. Judges 8:22, 24 seems to equate Midianites with Ishmaelites, so the Torah was probably speaking here of a single group, not two distinct ones.

---

[35] Alter notes in a footnote here: "This is precisely the verb used for Hagar (21:15) when she flings Ishmael under a bush in the wilderness."

[36] Alter, *Genesis: Translation and Commentary*, 212.

[37] Sacks, *Covenant & Conversation*, 275.

A particularly chilling detail is highlighted in this narrative. Once they had stripped Joseph of his clothes and thrown him into the pit, they calmly sat down to break bread and to have a meal. The Hebrew וַיֵּשְׁבוּ לֶאֱכָל־לֶחֶם (va-yeshvu le-ekhal lechem) literally means "and they sat down to eat bread" (vs. 25). When the brothers go to Egypt many years later, they will do so to buy *grain for bread* from none other than Joseph. When Reuben returned and realized that his plan had failed and that his young brother had already been sent off, he grieved, but joined his brothers in their conspiracy of keeping secret what had really happened to Joseph (Gen. 37:29-31).

## Deceiving Jacob

וַיִּקְחוּ אֶת־כְּתֹנֶת יוֹסֵף וַיִּשְׁחֲטוּ שְׂעִיר עִזִּים וַיִּטְבְּלוּ אֶת־הַכֻּתֹּנֶת בַּדָּם: וַיְשַׁלְּחוּ אֶת־
כְּתֹנֶת הַפַּסִּים וַיָּבִיאוּ אֶל־אֲבִיהֶם וַיֹּאמְרוּ זֹאת מָצָאנוּ הַכֶּר־נָא הַכְּתֹנֶת בִּנְךָ הִוא אִם־
לֹא:

*So they took Joseph's tunic, killed a young goat, and dipped the tunic in the blood. Then they brought the special tunic to their father and said, "We found this. Determine now whether it is your son's tunic or not." (Gen. 37:31-32)*

Jacob, once the master of trickery and manipulation, becomes the deceived in this story. He falsely concludes exactly what the conspiring brothers hoped he would think. We read in Hebrew that חַיָּה רָעָה אֲכָלָתְהוּ טָרֹף טֹרַף יוֹסֵף (chayah raah akhalathu tarof taraf Yosef), which literally translated means "a wicked animal ate him; Joseph was truly torn up." The story underscores the irony of being deceived in a very similar way as one has deceived in the past. First Laban substituted sisters to trick Jacob at the moment he lowered his guard. Now, just as Jacob had used a slaughtered kid and his brother's clothes in the deception of his father many years earlier, so do his sons in implying the fate of Joseph.

Thus Genesis 37 ends with Jacob's inconsolable grief over the loss of Joseph. He is so convinced that Joseph is dead and his body fully devoured, that he does not even order a search for his remains. All the years that Joseph was in Egyptian exile, Jacob suffered from tremendous emotional pain such that his life was defined by grief over the loss of Joseph. As Israel wailed over Joseph, the merchants sold him to Potiphar in Egypt.

## The Judah Interruption

Highlighting that the so-called "Joseph story" is not only about Joseph, the text is suddenly interrupted by a story about Judah's moral failure in withholding from Tamar the benefit of a levirate marriage (Deut. 25:5-6). It is as if Judah's story was later inserted into the text to break up the drama. The custom of levirate marriage was simple. If a man died without any heirs, his brother was obligated to marry his widow, and her firstborn son would be considered as the offspring of the deceased brother. Thus his line lives on. After the death of his first son, Judah's second son married Tamar, but he refused to produce a son for his dead brother. As a result, the LORD took his life as a punishment.

Why such a harsh punishment? We read about it in Genesis 38. Judah's second son Onan, after each intercourse with Tamar, deliberately spilled his seed on the ground. Onan seems to have reasoned that if a child was born as a result of his sexual union with Tamar, not only would he have to spend his family resources on a child that did not legally belong to him, but he would also forfeit the right to his brother's inheritance as next in line.

He failed to act responsibly and righteously towards this community of faith that God was forming from the children of Jacob/Israel. When Onan died, Judah promised Tamar that when his third son was old enough to marry he would become her husband. But Judah did not honor his promise and did not act righteously as well. Judah's concern is understandable. Two of his sons already died while they were married to Tamar. Maybe something is wrong with her? He was afraid that the same fate would befall his youngest child. Even though the chapter seems oddly placed, Judah's moral failure in withholding his youngest son from Tamar ties back in some important ways to the Abraham, Isaac and Jacob narratives, as well as to the main drama of Joseph and his brothers. Joseph was the youngest (except Benjamin) and most treasured.

Tamar was desperate and took matters into her own hands. She determined that her father-in-law's unfaithfulness will not stop her from having children and being a part of God's family. Tamar pretends to be a prostitute. Judah, after a period of mourning (his wife had died some time ago), seeks a one-time sexual service from a (presumed) prostitute who unknown to him, is actually Tamar in disguise. Tamar becomes pregnant and when the news of Tamar's extra-marital pregnancy became known to Judah, he harshly condemned her to death. When he was presented with his personal items, given to the prostitute as a pledge, he had a change of heart. (Gen. 38:24-26).

When Tamar showed Judah's personal items to him she said in Hebrew הַכֶּר־נָא (haker na) "please examine" (vs. 25). Ironically these are the exact same words Judah and the brothers said to Israel, הַכֶּר־נָא (haker na) "please examine" (Gen 37:32), while showing him Joseph's torn clothes. Judah's deception returned to him in his own words.

What is striking to most modern readers is that Tamar's action of pretending to be a prostitute is not exactly condemned in any way. There is no condemnation of Judah's use of a prostitute either. Rather, the focus of Torah's text is on Judah's sin of mistreating Tamar. One interpretation is that this demonstrates that the overall concern of the chapter (and probably by extension the entire story of Jacob's children) is focused not on individual purity of life, but on communal responsibility towards the well-being of a group. What was asked of Judah was "that he risk his son for the sake of the community, that he make his son, even his last son, available for the

70

solidarity and future of the community now focused in the person of this defenseless widow."[38]

Unrighteous/unjust behaviors are not viewed as merely personal failings, but communal issues. "What is taken most seriously is not a violation of sexual convention, but damage to the community which includes a poor, diminished female."[39] The story of Tamar and Judah seems to operate according to the principle: "From one to whom much is given, much is required." Tamar had the right to a child by the nearest of kin of her dead husband. The right was deliberately withheld from her. Judah later repented of his action:

צָדְקָה מִמֶּנִּי כִּי־עַל־כֵּן לֹא־נְתַתִּיהָ לְשֵׁלָה בְנִי וְלֹא־יָסַף עוֹד לְדַעְתָּהּ

*"She is more in the right than I, inasmuch as I did not give her to my son Shelah." And he was not intimate with her again. (Gen. 38:26b).*

After Tamar became pregnant with the twin children of Judah (Perez and Zerah), Judah does not approach her sexually again. This is a very important observation and a point that the writer/compiler(s) of Torah narrative seek(s) to communicate. Yes, Judah is a man of flawed character. Like others, he sometimes does things that are both unwise and plainly wrong. But he is Jacob/Israel's true son. Like Jacob, Judah is a man who is able to "own" his guilt, thereby chartering a new repentant course for his future. Judah's destiny will soon become clear. It is his family that will lead Israel, bringing forth the quintessential Israelite King (Gen. 49:8-10) in the person of David, who himself will exhibit both Judah's vices and his virtues.

While the story of Ruth (the great-grandmother of David) occurs much later in history, there are a number of very strong connections between Tamar and Ruth. They are both widows who bear children to older relatives. Another important point to note is that both are found in the genealogy of King David, the Israelite King, who was a

---

[38] Brueggemann, *Genesis: Interpretation*, 310.
[39] *Ibid.*, 311.

descendant of the tribe of Judah. The medieval Jewish Kabbalistic work called the Zohar observes this similarity in the following summary:

> There were two women – Tamar and Ruth – from whom the line of Judah was built, and from whom issued King David, King Solomon, and the Messiah. These two women were similar: after their first husbands died, they made efforts to win their second husbands. In doing so, both of them acted properly for the sake of kindness to the dead [by bearing children who would perpetuate their memory]." (Zohar 1:188b)

The parallels between Tamar and Ruth are extensive and deserve more recognition than the brief reference that the Zohar affords them. The importance of their roles is clear: both are joined together and both anticipate the Lion from the Tribe of Judah who will one day rise up to govern Israel and the entire world (Gen. 49:8-12).

**Potiphar's Trust**

As chapter 38 ends, the story returns to Joseph in Potiphar's house. Verse 2 is a key phrase establishing the connection between the LORD God's faithfulness to Joseph with His faithfulness to Jacob in preceding narratives:

וַיְהִי יהוה אֶת־יוֹסֵף וַיְהִי אִישׁ מַצְלִיחַ

*And the LORD was with Joseph, and he was a successful man (Gen. 39:2).*

The personal presence of the LORD God was with Joseph. It did not matter where Joseph found himself. It did not matter if the circumstances were good or bad. God was with him. It was the "LORD being with him" that brought the preordained result – Joseph was a successful man, much like Abraham, Isaac and Jacob before him. Potiphar, who himself worked in the court of the Pharaoh of Egypt knew what it was to do work with excellence. He knew success when he saw it. It was because of this excellence and success in virtually everything Joseph did, that Potiphar took favorable notice of him. He promoted Joseph, appointing him as steward over everything he owned (Gen. 39:4). We read in Genesis 39:5-6.

וַיְהִי מֵאָז הִפְקִיד אֹתוֹ בְּבֵיתוֹ וְעַל כָּל־אֲשֶׁר יֶשׁ־לוֹ וַיְבָרֶךְ יהוה אֶת־בֵּית הַמִּצְרִי בִּגְלַל יוֹסֵף וַיְהִי בִּרְכַּת יהוה בְּכָל־אֲשֶׁר יֶשׁ־לוֹ בַּבַּיִת וּבַשָּׂדֶה

*And from the time that the Egyptian put him in charge of his household and of all that he owned, the LORD blessed his house for Joseph's sake, so that the blessing of the LORD was upon everything that he owned, in the house and outside. (Gen. 39:5)*

The story of Joseph shows one thing very clearly. The LORD of the covenant is committed to being faithful to Jacob's children also. The blessing of Abraham that was confirmed upon Jacob included his children, whether or not they resided in the Promised Land. Just as God said that the nations that bless Abraham will themselves be blessed, so we see the outworking of this blessing in the life of Joseph, the descendant of Abraham, Isaac and Jacob.

The Hebrew says וַיְבָרֶךְ יהוה אֶת־בֵּית הַמִּצְרִי בִּגְלַל יוֹסֵף *(va-yevarekh YHWH et bet ha-mitsri biglal Yosef)*, which translated means that "the LORD blessed the house of the Egyptian because of Joseph." Using the Hebrew parallelism technique of stating the same thought differently and expanding it a little, the text continues וַיְהִי בִּרְכַּת יהוה בְּכָל־אֲשֶׁר יֶשׁ־לוֹ בַּבַּיִת וּבַשָּׂדֶה *(va-yhi birkat YHWH be-khol asher yesh lo ba-bayit u-va-sadeh)*, which translated means that "the LORD blessed everything that belonged to him, (whether) in the house or in the field." The blessing of God that came to this Egyptian household was overwhelming, and it was all because of Joseph.

A very similar situation had occurred in the life of Jacob while he was living and working with Laban. In Genesis 30:27 we read that God blessed Laban because of Jacob's presence in his house. This is a deliberate parallel between Israel and Joseph. To state it more precisely, the blessings were all because of God's promise to Abraham, Isaac and Jacob and their posterity.

73

וַיַּעֲזֹב כָּל־אֲשֶׁר־לוֹ בְּיַד־יוֹסֵף וְלֹא־יָדַע אִתּוֹ מְאוּמָה כִּי אִם־הַלֶּחֶם אֲשֶׁר־הוּא אוֹכֵל וַיְהִי יוֹסֵף יְפֵה־תֹאַר וִיפֵה מַרְאֶה

*He left all that he had in Joseph's hands and, with him there, he paid attention to nothing save the food that he ate. Now Joseph was well built and handsome. (Gen. 39:6)*

Potiphar entrusted everything to Joseph with the exception of just one thing – the food he ate. While Potiphar saw that Joseph was extremely successful in everything he did, Joseph was still a foreign slave and someone who was, according to Egyptian religious customs, ceremonially unclean and therefore could not be involved in the preparation of food. At the end of the narrative when Joseph's brothers are not allowed to eat together with the Egyptians, we will clearly see why (Gen. 43:32). Egyptians, like the Israelites, did not view the matters of food consumption as mundane – they belonged to the realm of the sacred. The thought that such economic refugees or migrants could have anything to do with the realm of the sacred, no matter how mundane this encounter seemed to everyone around, never entered his mind.

However, there may have been another reason as well. Potiphar is called שַׂר הַטַּבָּחִים (*sar ha-tabachim*), which could be translated as "the chief of the cooks" or also "the chief of the bodyguards" – or literally even "executioners" (Gen. 37:36). If the job of Potiphar was to provide security to the Pharaoh of Egypt, then it would have included security over the food he consumed. A primary way to remove any unwanted king from his throne throughout history has been to poison him. So, in this case, Potiphar's job would have predisposed him to put Joseph in charge of everything in the household except the matters of food. This job could not be entrusted into the hands of a foreign national. It was just too dangerous. It is, of course, ironic that years later Pharaoh will appoint Joseph to be his right-hand man in all Egypt. Joseph will then administer the matters of food on behalf of the entire nation of

Egypt as well as the surrounding world that will come to find bread in Egypt.

## Joseph's Temptation

Potiphar was not the only one who took a liking to Joseph. His wife was also attracted to him. He was young, handsome, and incredibly successful. Perhaps she saw far more of him than she did of her own husband. As the text testifies, one of the character traits of Joseph was his loyalty. Acting as a true Israelite, he guarded Potiphar's *honor* just as he guarded everything else in Potiphar's house. Everything that belonged to Potiphar, was Potiphar's, and that included his unfaithful wife. When Joseph spoke to Potiphar's wife attempting to dissuade her from her continual sexual harassment, among other things, he said the following about Potiphar:

אֵינֶנּוּ גָדוֹל בַּבַּיִת הַזֶּה מִמֶּנִּי וְלֹא־חָשַׂךְ מִמֶּנִּי מְאוּמָה כִּי אִם־אוֹתָךְ בַּאֲשֶׁר אַתְּ־אִשְׁתּוֹ וְאֵיךְ אֶעֱשֶׂה הָרָעָה הַגְּדֹלָה הַזֹּאת וְחָטָאתִי לֵאלֹהִים

*He wields no more authority in this house than I, and he has withheld nothing from me except yourself, since you are his wife. How then could I do this most wicked thing, and sin before God?" (Gen. 39:9).*

There are two reasons that held Joseph back from succumbing to the temptations of Potiphar's wife. First, Joseph's gratitude to Potiphar for the trust he placed in him. Literally, the Hebrew says, אֵינֶנּוּ גָדוֹל בַּבַּיִת הַזֶּה מִמֶּנִּי (*eynenu gadol ba-bayit ha-zeh mi-meni*), which means "there is no one greater than me in this house." Joseph was greatly honored by Potiphar. To use his willing wife for sexual pleasure would have violated this trusting relationship at its core. Like Adam in the Garden of Eden, there was only one thing that was strictly forbidden to Joseph in Potiphar's house. Adam failed by eating from the only tree that was forbidden to him; whereas Joseph succeeded by avoiding sexual contact with the one woman who was forbidden to him. Joseph, as a true son of Abraham, Isaac and Jacob, must not fail where their ancestor Adam did.

The second reason was based upon Joseph's awareness of God's presence with him. The God of Abraham, Isaac and Jacob was not merely a territorial god like many others in the minds of ancient people. He supervised the affairs of the entire world. This meant that Joseph (who was no doubt taught by Jacob/Israel about his God), was convinced that whether he was in the Land of Canaan or in Egypt, or whether he was in a public place or in the locked chambers of Potiphar, God was present there as well. God was with him, not only in his success and prosperity, but also in moments of great temptation and responsibility. God being with him was not simply Joseph's magic power to be righteous, but also his moral compass that provided guidance.

## Joseph's Faithfulness

Joseph resisted the temptation. Unlike Judah in Chapter 38, Joseph is praised for upholding community values and seeking its greater good at the expense of his own discomfort (the opposite to Judah's actions towards Tamar). Joseph does so in a foreign land, in a community to which he does not really belong. One intent in these stories is simple – community is of utmost importance in the sight of God. Jacob's covenant children must learn to behave in selfless ways. God is building not just a family, but a nation. The nation of Israel which will emerge from Jacob's children cannot follow the path of Cain. It must become a holy people, a kingdom of priests. In Exodus 19:5-6 we read: "Now then, if you will obey Me faithfully and keep My covenant, you shall be My treasured possession among all the peoples. Indeed, all the earth is Mine, but you shall be to Me a kingdom of priests and a holy nation. These are the words that you shall speak to the children of Israel." (Ex. 19:5-6)

After repeated unsuccessful attempts to persuade Joseph to sleep with her, Potiphar's wife accused the innocent Joseph of attempted rape – apparently out of a sense of disappointment, anger and vengeance. He denied the charges, but Potiphar just could not overlook his own wife's accusation.[40] So, ignoring the plea of Joseph and taking the accuser's circumstantial evidence as sufficient, Potiphar placed Joseph in the prison where Egyptians sentenced by the Pharaoh himself were held indefinitely (Gen. 39:11-20). It is possible that Potiphar suspected something and did not believe his wife either. He did not want to kill Joseph, just in case he was innocent. And at the same time he wanted to remove Joseph from his wife, and so Joseph was imprisoned. It should not come as a surprise to us that the LORD's presence could not be held back by the prison doors. We read in Genesis 39:21 that "the LORD was with Joseph" וַיְהִי יהוה אֶת־יוֹסֵף *(va-yehi YHWH et Yosef)*.

## Interpreting Dreams

The next section of the narrative begins with Pharaoh's displeasure with his מַשְׁקֶה *(mishkeh)* "cup bearer" and אֹפֶה *(ofeh)* "baker" who served in his royal court. Pharaoh puts both of these main servants into jail, probably pending an investigation about what really took place on their watch. They end up in the same prison as Joseph. Just as Joseph quickly found favor with Potiphar, he also found favor with the jailer. Joseph was given duties in the jail house and the jailer trusted him with taking care of prisoners because he was successful in everything he did. Multiple times we read that the Lord was with Joseph and he is the one who gave him favor with people and success.

As providence would have it, given their high status as the king's servants, Joseph was assigned to take care of them. Both of

---

[40] There is one other point that should be made. There existed in Egypt a tale of two brothers who lived and work together. The wife of one of the brothers sought to seduce him, but the other brother refused, remaining faithful. She accused him of rape and the brother, believing her to be a victim, sought his brother's death. God helped the fleeing brother, who eventually died, and after series of what seems to our modern ear of bizarre events, is resurrected and is able to impregnate his wife, producing posterity. It is likely that both Potiphar and Joseph, and especially Israelites that left the land of Egypt, were very familiar with this story. What connection (if any) may have existed between this story and the story of Joseph and Potiphar is not clear. "The Tale of the two Brothers Anpu and Bata," http://www.reshafim.org.il/ad/egypt/texts/anpu_and_bata.htm (accessed January 3, 2016).

Pharaoh's servants dreamt disturbing dreams at night. Because they were in prison, they had no access to priests. There were no professional dream interpreters around for them to seek explanations. The logic of ancient people was simple: if the gods are trying to tell them something, but they don't understand, they could end up displeasing the gods further by their actions. This is a very undesirable result for men who are already in jail. In the morning Joseph finds them perplexed and they share their problem with Joseph. Joseph assures them that his all-present God is certainly capable to interpret their dreams.

הֲלוֹא לֵאלֹהִים פִּתְרֹנִים סַפְּרוּ-נָא לִי:

*"Surely God can interpret! Tell me." (Gen. 40:8)*

Alter explains, "In Egypt, the interpretation of dreams was regarded as a science, and formal instruction in techniques of dream interpretation was given in schools called 'houses of life.'"[41] Joseph tells these men that the Egyptian idea about dreams is wrong. God is perfectly capable to interpret dreams and give the interpretation to those not considered "experts." The chief cupbearer tells Joseph the details of his dream. Joseph interprets it to mean that in three days the Pharaoh will free him and he will be restored to his service in the same honorable position. The chief baker tells Joseph the details of his dream. Joseph interprets it to mean that in three days the chief baker will be executed by hanging. Both interpretations of the dreams come true exactly in the way Joseph interpreted them. (Gen. 40:9-13). Interestingly, when Joseph told his dreams to his family there was no need to interpret them. Jacob and his sons understood the dreams perfectly. But Egyptians needed interpretation.

## Joseph is Forgotten

After Joseph interpreted the meaning of the dream to the chief cupbearer, he asked him something that at the time the cupbearer

---

41 Alter, *Genesis: Translation and Commentary*, 230.

probably did not pay much attention to. Joseph asked that when the cupbearer finds himself free again in the service of the king, that he would tell Pharaoh about Joseph's fate (Gen. 40:14-15). Understandably or, perhaps, even conveniently, the cupbearer forgot about Joseph when he was freed. As readers or hearers of the story grow in their sympathy towards Joseph, it is with great pain that they hear about the cupbearer's forgetfulness. We read in Gen. 40:23:

וְלֹא־זָכַר שַׂר־הַמַּשְׁקִים אֶת־יוֹסֵף וַיִּשְׁכָּחֵהוּ

*Yet the chief cupbearer did not think of Joseph; he forgot him. (Gen. 40:23)*

The Torah uses phrases like לֹא־זָכַר (*lo zakhar*), which means "did not remember" and יִּשְׁכָּחֵהוּ (*yishkachehu*), which means "forgot about him." Both phrases restate and reinforce the same exact concept – Joseph was not remembered. This concept is set in opposition to the familiar idea of God's remembrance of Noah, Lot and Rachel. When Noah, his family and his animals were drifting in the boat amidst the flood, the Hebrew texts states that יִזְכֹּר אֱלֹהִים אֶת־נֹחַ (*yizkor Elohim et Noach*) "God remembered Noah." God spared Lot from being judged together with the evil inhabitants of Sodom and Gomorrah because He remembered Abraham (Gen. 19:29). The Hebrew phraseology in that case is remarkably similar to the case of God remembering Noah: יִזְכֹּר אֱלֹהִים אֶת־אַבְרָהָם (*yizkor Elohim et Avraham*). When Leah bore Jacob six sons and one daughter while Rachel remained barren in utter distress, we are told in Hebrew יִזְכֹּר אֱלֹהִים אֶת־רָחֵל (*yizkor Elohim et Rachel*) - "God remembered Rachel."

In all the scenarios, Noah, Lot and Rachel, whom God remembered, were very much in need of God's salvation. They were in need of a relief from their misfortunes. This particular phraseology also looks forward to God remembering the children of Abraham, Isaac and Jacob in Egyptian captivity and being willing to act on their behalf, leading them out of the land of their slavery (Ex. 2:24; 6:5). The "God remembered" phraseology in reality functions as a synonym for "God acted on behalf of someone." When God remembered

Noah, the waters of the flood receded. When God remembered Abraham, his nephew Lot was taken to safety. When God remembered Rachel, he opened up her womb. By the same token, when the chief cupbearer "forgot" and "did not remember," the statements simply signified his inaction.

This does not necessarily mean that the cupbearer literally forgot Joseph or his request. The chief cupbearer most likely remembered Joseph's request, but for some reason he chose not to act upon it. The cupbearer never told Pharaoh about Joseph. Perhaps it was too risky, considering how close he came to death the last time when Pharaoh was displeased with his servants. This lack of action on the part of the cupbearer would cost Joseph two more full years of life in jail. The emphasis is on the length of the wait in Torah. This is probably why the emphatic Hebrew phrase שְׁנָתַיִם יָמִים (*shenatayim yamim*), which literally means "two years of days," was used. It expressed the fullness of time. When God directs the events in people's lives they happen exactly when they need to occur.

## Pharaoh's Dreams

The Pharaoh dreamed two dreams. They were strange and Pharaoh, just like the chief cupbearer and chief baker, was truly distressed about their meaning (Gen. 41:8). It was the duty of the Pharaoh of Egypt to ensure the tranquility and prosperity of the Land. So obviously the contents of the dreams got Pharaoh really worried. The next morning his spirit was agitated and he sent for all the magicians of Egypt, and all its wise men. Pharaoh told them his dreams, but none could interpret them for Pharaoh. The chief cupbearer and chief baker were distressed in the previous story because there was no professional interpreter of dreams around in the jail house, but Pharaoh had them at his disposal.

The ineptness of the Egyptian priesthood becomes obvious. Everyone was called in but no one was capable to provide a certain answer. Pharaoh was at a loss. "The monopoly of knowledge in the empire is broken. Pharaoh knows many things. He knows how to manage and administer and control. As we may see in the Exodus narrative, he knows how to prosper and how to oppress. But he does not know how to discern the movement of God's way within his realm. Only God knows that."[42] Only then does the chief cupbearer find the courage to speak to the Pharaoh about a Hebrew slave locked up in his prison (Gen. 41:9-13). The suggestion is still risky, but now it seems fully justified since everyone has failed to interpret the dreams and Pharaoh is still upset. Without much delay Pharaoh orders Joseph to be brought from the dungeon into his presence. The dungeon in Genesis 41:14 is called בּוֹר *(bor)* "pit." This is the exact same word as used in Genesis 37: 24 to describe the dried-up well that Joseph's brothers used to confine him.

Once Joseph was cleaned up and prepared to enter the King's presence he was ushered in without much delay. His head was shaved and new clothes were given to him (Gen.41:14). "In the ancient Near East, only the Egyptians were clean-shaven, and the verb used here can equally refer to shaving the head, or close-cropping it, another distinctive Egyptian practice."[43] The new garments on Joseph were probably necessary, but the listeners of the story are probably meant to remember also all the stories of Joseph's garments. His special garment got him into trouble with his brothers. It was taken from him and dipped in blood to deceive his father. Joseph's garment was used by Potiphar's wife to accuse him. Each time Joseph was mistreated and thrown into a dark place his garment was taken from him. Now a garment is restored to him. When Pharaoh elevates him (later in the story), Joseph will receive another special garment worthy of an Egyptian aristocrat and ruler.

The story moves quickly and the next scene begins with the Pharaoh himself retelling Joseph the content of his first dream. We read in Genesis 41:15-16 that Pharaoh said to Joseph:

---

[42] Brueggemann, *Genesis: Interpretation*, 322.
[43] Alter, *Genesis: Translation and Commentary*, 236.

חֲלוֹם חָלַמְתִּי וּפֹתֵר אֵין אֹתוֹ וַאֲנִי שָׁמַעְתִּי עָלֶיךָ לֵאמֹר תִּשְׁמַע חֲלוֹם לִפְתֹּר אֹתוֹ

*"I have had a dream, but no one can interpret it. Now I have heard it said of you that for you to hear a dream is to tell its meaning." (Gen. 41:15)*

וַיַּעַן יוֹסֵף אֶת־פַּרְעֹה לֵאמֹר בִּלְעָדָי אֱלֹהִים יַעֲנֶה אֶת־שְׁלוֹם פַּרְעֹה

*Joseph answered Pharaoh, saying, "Not I! God will see to Pharaoh's welfare."
(Gen. 41:16)*

Pharaoh received a report that Joseph possesses an extraordinary ability to interpret dreams. Joseph, however, responds that "only God himself" בִּלְעָדָי אֱלֹהִים *(biladay Elohim)* will answer regarding the שָׁלוֹם *(shalom)* "well-being" of Pharaoh. It is possible that Joseph's refusal to claim that he interprets dreams himself has to do with the divinity claims of the Pharaoh himself. For Joseph, the Pharaoh was not divine. It would be God who will answer Pharaoh. So Joseph says that he is not the source of interpretation.

When Pharaoh told Joseph that exact content of both dreams, Joseph told him that the two dreams are really the same one dream repeated. The meaning of the dreams is that God has decided to show Pharaoh His plans for the next 14 years. The double dreaming confirms the irreversibility of this message and that it is imminent. It will surely come to pass (Gen. 41:25-32). The dream, in fact, was a sign of God's favor upon Pharaoh and upon Egypt. Now that the Pharaoh has been informed of God's plans, preparations could be made to avoid an economic catastrophe. While providing the interpretation, Joseph also suggested a plan to Pharaoh – the purposeful and consistent saving of extra grain that will be received in the next seven coming harvest seasons to insure future prosperity (Gen. 41:33-36).

## Joseph is Elevated

When Pharaoh took council with his royal advisors, all agreed that Joseph can be put in charge of this project effective immediately (Gen. 41:37-38). Pharaoh made Joseph the second man in Egypt, stating that only Pharaoh's throne will separate the authority of Joseph from that of Pharaoh.

We read in Genesis 41:40:

אַתָּה תִּהְיֶה עַל־בֵּיתִי וְעַל־פִּיךָ יִשַּׁק כָּל־עַמִּי רַק הַכִּסֵּא אֶגְדַּל מִמֶּךָ

*You shall be in charge of my court, and by your command shall all my people be directed; only with respect to the throne shall I be superior to you." (Gen. 41:40)*

The Hebrew אַתָּה תִּהְיֶה עַל־בֵּיתִי *(atah tihyeh al beti)* literally means "you will be over my house" and עַל־פִּיךָ יִשַּׁק כָּל־עַמִּי *(al pikha yishek kol ami)*, which is very difficult to translate literally, perhaps means something like "over your mouth/according to you will all people kiss [i.e., be ruled]." Pharaoh's words were not empty. He proceeded to grant Joseph formal authority in Egypt. Joseph will govern Egypt in every way but just coming short of being Pharaoh. These words reflect the state of things that had been at Potiphar's house. Joseph had had responsibility over almost all of Potiphar's affairs (Gen. 49:4).

וַיֹּאמֶר פַּרְעֹה אֶל־יוֹסֵף רְאֵה נָתַתִּי אֹתְךָ עַל כָּל־אֶרֶץ מִצְרָיִם

*Pharaoh further said to Joseph, "See, I put you in charge of all the land of Egypt." (Gen. 41:41)*

וַיָּסַר פַּרְעֹה אֶת־טַבַּעְתּוֹ מֵעַל יָדוֹ וַיִּתֵּן אֹתָהּ עַל־יַד יוֹסֵף וַיַּלְבֵּשׁ אֹתוֹ בִּגְדֵי־שֵׁשׁ
וַיָּשֶׂם רְבִד הַזָּהָב עַל־צַוָּארוֹ

*And removing his signet ring from his hand, Pharaoh put it on Joseph's hand; and he had him dressed in robes of fine linen, and put a gold chain about his neck. (Gen. 41:42)*

This time Pharaoh not only speaks but acts. He officially confers the high office upon Joseph and confirms this by adorning the Hebrew slave with the regal insignia. Joseph receives the signet ring, the golden collar, and the fine linen dress. Based on Egyptian frescos the "golden chain" should be understood as an Egyptian ornamental collar instead.[44] Pharaoh had Joseph ride in the chariot of his second-in-command, and they cried before him, "Abrek!" Thus he placed him over all the land of Egypt. "The narrative reflects the firm authority of Joseph. He is clearly in charge. None may resist or question... As the story develops, there is a ruthlessness which makes survival possible. There is also remarkable technical "know-how" put at the service of imperial well-being."[45]

Pharaoh summarized the level of authority that he granted to Joseph by stating in Genesis 41:44:

אֲנִי פַרְעֹה וּבִלְעָדֶיךָ לֹא־יָרִים אִישׁ אֶת־יָדוֹ וְאֶת־רַגְלוֹ בְּכָל־אֶרֶץ מִצְרָיִם

*"I am Pharaoh; (yet) without you, no one shall lift up hand or foot in all the land of Egypt." (Gen. 41:44)*

Alter writes, "Most commentators and translators have construed this as an implied antithesis: though I am Pharaoh, without you no man shall raise hand or foot... But this is unnecessary because we know that royal decrees in the ancient Near East regularly began with the formula: I am King X. The sense here would thus be: By the authority of the Pharaoh, I declare that without you..."[46] It is interesting that the same phraseology בִלְעָדֶיךָ *(biladekha)* "without you" that is used in reference to Joseph by Pharaoh, was used by Joseph to say that "only God" could interpreted Pharaoh's dreams בִּלְעָדַי אֱלֹהִים *(biladi Elohim)*. It is possible that the use of this phrase is intentional. The Torah writer may be drawing a connection here

44   Alter, *Genesis: Translation and Commentary*, 240.
45   Brueggemann, *Genesis: Interpretation*, 328.
46   Alter, *Genesis: Translation and Commentary*, 240.

between Joseph's complete reliance and honor of God and Pharaoh honoring of Joseph with great authority in Egypt.

Another commentator adds: "Joseph will indeed rule, just as his brothers feared (Gen. 37.8, 10 - 11), but with this crucial qualification: His rule will be rooted not in sheer power, but in the benefit he provides to the less fortunate. This corresponds to an ideal of kingship widespread in the ancient Near East, in which the king is the rescuer and servant of the people."[47] As a sign of Joseph's new identity Pharaoh gave Joseph a new name. He called him Zaphenath-Paneah (צָפְנַת פַּעְנֵחַ). Although there is no agreement among Egyptologists as to what this name may actually mean, one fitting, but only possible suggestion is that צָפְנַת פַּעְנֵחַ is a Hebrew transliteration of Egyptian for "God speaks, he lives." In Gen. 42:6 Joseph's brothers bowed to him, and Hebrew uses the same verb for this act as in Gen. 37:9-10 where Joseph's dreams are described.

Pharaoh also gives him Asenath אָסְנַת *(Osnat)*, a daughter of Poti-Phera priest of On, as a wife. The association of Poti-Phera, a priest of the city of On with Potiphar of Pharaoh's court is unlikely. While Asenath's name translated from Egyptian means "the one belonging to Neith (goddess)," in Jewish tradition we witness the transformation of Asenath into a faithful convert to Judaism. Of course, only in prototype, since the peculiar Jewish way of life, national identity and tradition for conversion itself would be developed much later in history. Suffice it to say that Asenath is regarded as having accepted the faith and the ways of her husband, and Joseph's children were deemed true descendants of Jacob. This of course follows the biblical patrilineal pattern of heritage (vs. the later rabbinic matrilineal system). Moses, by the way, also married a daughter of a Gentile priest. He was also rejected by his own, but became a great leader and redeemer of his people. In the case of

---

[47] Levenson, "Genesis Introductions and Annotations," *The Jewish Study Bible*, ed. Berlin and Brettler, 77.

Joseph, it is clear that the covenant of Abraham, Isaac and Jacob was continued through Manasseh and Ephraim, Asenath's children.

Asenath's story would later be told in a Jewish book from the Hellenistic era called *Joseph and Asenath*. This book attempted to resolve the unspoken tension of Asenath in Joseph's life. Authored probably sometime around the first century CE, the twenty-some chapter work speaks about the transformation of Asenath the idol-worshiper to a worshiper of Israel's God. The imaginative story provides a window into the world of Jewish thinking about conversion at the time of its composition. Of course, the book was written many centuries after Torah and adds no real historical value to the understanding of the original story of Joseph and Asenath.

Joseph was roughly thirty years old when all of these things took place (Gen. 41:26). His new job involved a lot of traveling. He was supervising the entirety of Egypt to reach a very important point – enough provisions saved to survive a regional famine. Just as everything prior that Joseph put his hand to, this nationwide project was also destined for great success. In Genesis 41:38 Pharaoh asks a rhetorical question:

הֲנִמְצָא כָזֶה אִישׁ אֲשֶׁר רוּחַ אֱלֹהִים בּוֹ

*"Could we find another like him, a man in whom is the spirit of God?" (Gen. 41:38)*

Almost identical words were said about a craftsman named Bezalel in Exodus 31:2. It is ironic that Joseph's family did not recognize (or admit) these traits in him, but Pharaoh did. "The Egyptian monarch has not been turned into a monotheist by Joseph, but he has gone along with Joseph's idea that human wisdom is a gift of God, or the gods, and the expression he uses could have the rather general force of 'divine spirit.'"[48] The ancient Egyptians and many other people of the Near East worshipped forces of nature, which they also personified as gods and depicted visually. Israel's neighbors were

---

[48]    Alter, *Genesis: Translation and Commentary*, 239.

known to refer to the divine as El, or Eloah. But the word El often meant a personified force, a power connected to the element of nature. "There is a fundamental difference between those belief-systems and Israelite faith. It held that the forces of nature were not independent and autonomous. They represented a single totality, one creative will, the author of all being.[49]

During the first seven years, Joseph's Egyptian wife Asenath bore him two sons. He called the firstborn son "Manasseh" מְנַשֶּׁה *(Menasheh)*, which translated means "(God) has caused me to forget" – כִּי־נַשַּׁנִי אֱלֹהִים *(ki nashani Elohim)* – the hardship of the past and my parental home. The second son's name has a more positive meaning, described in the text as "God made me fruitful." The meaning of Joseph's sons' names has to do with his awareness that it was God who set him free and made him fruitful in Egypt (Gen. 41:51-52). The fertility of all Israelites in the land of Egypt will eventually prove to be a mixed blessing, because it is precisely when the Israelites were very fertile that a new king arose over Egypt who did not know Joseph, and he enslaved the Israelites (Ex. 1:7- 8).

## Joseph Governs Egypt

As seven fruitful harvest years came to an end, it became obvious that Joseph was not a lunatic and that Pharaoh was right in appointing him to the task of setting aside massive quantities of food. When the whole region began to experience starvation, Egypt still had bread. At some point, however, Egyptians too began to experience a famine just like the other nations around them. When that took place, Pharaoh directed people to ask Joseph, by telling them to "do whatever he tells you" אֲשֶׁר־יֹאמַר לָכֶם תַּעֲשׂוּ *(asher yomar la-khem taasu)*. Joseph rationed out the previously collected grain to the Egyptians. The world around Egypt also entered the time of severe famine. Not only did Egyptians come to Joseph, but the rest of the Mediterranean world did, too. The hunger becomes

---

49    Sacks, *Covenant & Conversation*, 287.

unbearable for Joseph's family in Canaan. Everything was set in motion for the eventual meeting of Joseph with his brothers as well as of Joseph and his beloved father.

## Time to Go to Egypt

When it became clear that Egypt had a significant surplus of food that could be acquired by others, Jacob said to his sons to stop wasting time by looking at one another: "Just go and get us what our family needs, so that we may live and not die!" (Gen. 42:1-3). The language is ironic. Many years ago some brothers were ready to lead Joseph into a path of death and eventually send him to Egypt as a slave to live and not die. Now Joseph's father is sending them to Egypt so that the entirety of Jacob's family will live and not die. (Other than the irony of meaning, these words – live and not die – of course show the high urgency that Jacob placed on his words to his ten sons). Jacob did not send his youngest son Benjamin, Joseph's full brother, with them out of fear that he would lose the only son he still has from Rachel, so the first trip to Egypt they make without him. Once they arrived, the sons of Israel got into a long line of those who had also come to Egypt to get food (Gen. 42:5).

## The Brothers Bow Down to Joseph

The text reminds us, as if we had the chance to forget, that it was Joseph who was appointed a vizier of Egypt and that when the brothers came to pay homage they had to bow down to him personally. We read in Genesis 42:6, 8:

וְיוֹסֵף הוּא הַשַּׁלִּיט עַל־הָאָרֶץ הוּא הַמַּשְׁבִּיר לְכָל־עַם הָאָרֶץ וַיָּבֹאוּ אֲחֵי יוֹסֵף
וַיִּשְׁתַּחֲווּ־לוֹ אַפַּיִם אָרְצָה׃

*Now Joseph was the vizier of the land; it was he who dispensed rations to all the people of the land. And Joseph's brothers came and bowed low to him, with their faces to the ground. (Gen. 42:6).*

וַיַּרְא יוֹסֵף אֶת־אֶחָיו וַיַּכִּרֵם וַיִּתְנַכֵּר אֲלֵיהֶם וַיְדַבֵּר אִתָּם קָשׁוֹת וַיֹּאמֶר אֲלֵהֶם מֵאַיִן בָּאתֶם וַיֹּאמְרוּ מֵאֶרֶץ כְּנַעַן לִשְׁבָּר־אֹכֶל:

*When Joseph saw his brothers, he recognized them; but he acted like a stranger toward them and spoke harshly to them. He asked them, "Where do you come from?" And they said, "From the land of Canaan, to procure food." (Gen. 42:7).*

וַיַּכֵּר יוֹסֵף אֶת־אֶחָיו וְהֵם לֹא הִכִּרֻהוּ:

*For though Joseph recognized his brothers, they did not recognize him. (Gen. 42:8).*

The English expression "to bow down" does not clearly communicate the idea of full prostration practiced in the Ancient Near East and inferred here by the use of the Hebrew וַיִּשְׁתַּחֲווּ־לוֹ *(va-yishtachavu lo)*, which basically means "and they prostrated themselves to him." "The verb for "recognize" (וַיַּכִּרֵם) and the verb for 'play the stranger' (וַיִּתְנַכֵּר אֲלֵיהֶם) are derived from the same root (the latter being a reflexive form of the root). Both uses pick up the thematically prominent repetition of the same root earlier in the story: Jacob was asked to 'recognize' Joseph's blood-soaked tunic and Tamar invited Judah to 'recognize' the tokens he had left with her as a security for payment for her sexual services."[50]

We will see later how the story of Judah and Tamar is intricately connected to the story of Joseph, but for now we see the linguistic hints here and there. The story simply mentions that he acted as a stranger towards them and spoke harshly to them: וַיְדַבֵּר אִתָּם קָשׁוֹת *(va-yedaber itam kashot)*. It is unlikely that at this time Joseph was already overwhelmed by a well-thought-through and appropriated sense of God's providential purposes and grace towards Israel's family and the world-at-large. This will certainly happen, but later. At this point Joseph is most likely rightfully angry with his flesh and blood about what they did to him, but his anger is, nevertheless,

---

50    Alter, *Genesis: Translation and Commentary*, 245.

constrained by a sense of God's presence with Joseph at all times and His goodness towards him.

## Joseph in Need of Grace

There is surely an element of sweet triumph for Joseph in seeing his grandiose dreams fulfilled so precisely, though it would be darkened by his recollection of what the report of his dreams led his brothers to do. As the brothers failed to recognize him, he certainly did not forget the looks of his offenders, even though they were now twenty years older. He only recalled the dreams that he had dreamt about them bowing down to him, that he was, no doubt, forced to reconsider many times over by the circumstances of his unfortunate captivity. "In chapter 37, he is a naive and guileless boy. In chapters 39-41, he is a noble and effective man of integrity who is not intimidated by the royal woman (39), the royal officers (40), nor even the Pharaoh (41). But in 42-44, he is now a ruthless and calculating governor. He understands the potential of his enormous office and exploits his capacity fully. He not only manipulates the scene but seems to relish his power to intimidate and threaten."[51]

In Genesis 42:9b we read of Joseph's accusation towards them as he sought to hide his identity from them:

וַיֹּאמֶר אֲלֵהֶם מְרַגְּלִים אַתֶּם לִרְאוֹת אֶת־עֶרְוַת הָאָרֶץ בָּאתֶם:

*He said to them, "You are spies, you have come to see the land in its nakedness." (Gen. 42:9b).*

The idiom refers to that which should be hidden from an outsider's eyes, as the nakedness of a human should be hidden from all but the legitimate sexual partner. The vizier is accusing the brothers of wanting to take advantage of Egypt's vulnerability, in some sense comparing it to a woman who can be overpowered and raped by a foreign evil-doer. The brothers argued that the assumptions of the

---

[51] Brueggemann, *Genesis: Interpretation*, 336-7.

vizier are baseless for the simple reason that all of them were brothers, the sons of the same father. The idea here being that the work of spies was a highly dangerous enterprise and it was unheard-of that the team of spies will be formed from an entire family. In the case of failure, the entire family will be dead. When they denied Joseph's accusations by stating that they were honest men, he restated his statement about their suspicious identity.

## A Demand to See the Brother

They said that they were once twelve brothers. They stated in Genesis 42:13b that:

וְהִנֵּה הַקָּטֹן אֶת־אָבִינוּ הַיּוֹם וְהָאֶחָד אֵינֶנּוּ׃

*Behold, the youngest is now with our father, and one is no more. (Gen. 42:13b).*

It is probably at this point in the story that, while Joseph still put up a harsh front, things in his heart may have begun very slowly to change from bitter hurt to eventual forgiveness, however far it was still from his heart. He told the brothers that in order to verify their story one of them would be allowed to go back to their father's house to bring their youngest brother to the Pharaoh, while all others would remain under arrest. He sent them into a jail house for three days to make sure that they saw how serious he was. On the third day he said to them something very interesting. We read in Genesis 42:18:

זֹאת עֲשׂוּ וִחְיוּ אֶת־הָאֱלֹהִים אֲנִי יָרֵא׃

*"Do this and you shall live, for I am a God-fearing man. (Gen. 42:18).*

He then told them that he was willing to change his previous verification test by allowing for only one to be kept captive with him and for the rest of them to go back to get their youngest brother. This made perfect sense. (Later on we will see a similar dynamic at play when Benjamin will be found riding with Joseph's silver cup in his sack). If the men were spies, they would not come back (after all they would not then be brothers but, rather, co-workers taking their own risks); but, if they were in Egypt on their stated business, they would certainly be able to do what was asked, especially now that the vizier was able to show them some leniency (Gen. 42:19-21).

The vizier's argument seemed believable to brothers. Joseph spoke to them through an interpreter and his incredible emotional self-control did not allow his brothers to know that he understood their every word. This sense of self-control will be lost completely when Judah, later in the narrative, begs Joseph to allow him to become a slave instead of Benjamin, Rachel's second son. It is at this point that Joseph will reveal himself to his brothers and weep out loud for all the neighbors to hear.

Already at this point in the narrative, a moment of truth has arrived. God has called them to an account. The brothers were convinced that they were being punished for their actions against Joseph many years earlier. We read in Genesis 42:21:

וַיֹּאמְרוּ אִישׁ אֶל־אָחִיו אֲבָל אֲשֵׁמִים אֲנַחְנוּ עַל־אָחִינוּ אֲשֶׁר רָאִינוּ צָרַת נַפְשׁוֹ בְּהִתְחַנְנוֹ אֵלֵינוּ וְלֹא שָׁמָעְנוּ עַל־כֵּן בָּאָה אֵלֵינוּ הַצָּרָה הַזֹּאת:

*"Alas, we are being punished on account of our brother, because we looked on at his anguish, yet paid no heed as he pleaded with us. That is why this distress has come upon us." (Gen. 42:21).*

וַיַּעַן רְאוּבֵן אֹתָם לֵאמֹר הֲלוֹא אָמַרְתִּי אֲלֵיכֶם לֵאמֹר אַל־תֶּחֶטְאוּ בַיֶּלֶד וְלֹא שְׁמַעְתֶּם וְגַם־דָּמוֹ הִנֵּה נִדְרָשׁ:

*Then Reuben spoke up and said to them, "Did I not tell you, 'Do no wrong to the boy'? But you paid no heed. Now comes the reckoning for his blood." (Gen. 42:22).*

Upon hearing these words, Joseph turned away, walked and wept in secret. In what seems almost like a fit of rage, Joseph came back to his brothers with his guards and arrested Simeon before their eyes.

He then gave orders to fill their bags with grain, reimburse them the money paid and to give them enough food for their journey. When the brothers later discovered that on the top of the grain the money that each one of them brought to Egypt to pay for the grain had been returned, their hearts sank.

## Bending under Pressure

An important series of disqualifying behaviors are recorded here to show that Reuben, in spite of being the firstborn son, would not be the leader of the future nation of Israel. It would be Judah who would take his role, and the later incorporation of Joseph's sons into the tribal count will further destabilize Reuben's communal standing. Reuben was too weak then to be a real leader, and he is too weak now. All he can do is to blame ("I told you so"), something that Joseph would not do in the end. This will be clearly contrasted with the responsible and brave actions of Judah (but more about that a bit later). Returning to their dismay at finding money in the grain sacks, Genesis 42:28b tells us of their words:

וַיֵּצֵא לִבָּם וַיֶּחֶרְדוּ אִישׁ אֶל־אָחִיו לֵאמֹר מַה־זֹּאת עָשָׂה אֱלֹהִים לָנוּ:

*Their hearts sank; and, trembling, they turned to one another, saying, "What is this that God has done to us?" (Gen. 42:28b).*

The Hebrew וַיֵּצֵא לִבָּם *(va-yetse libam)* literally means "and their hearts went out." They were truly afraid. They were no longer in control. When they arrived home, they told Jacob the entire truth about what had occurred during their journey (Gen. 42:29-35). "Because they could not believe the dream, they are forced to treat father Jacob as though he were the last generation who must be kept alive and unharmed for perpetuity. They cannot see themselves as a generation of promise-bearers."[52]

---

[52]    *Ibid.*, 338.

"The dream is happening. The future is at work toward life. But in their fearfulness, the brothers do not notice it."[53] The news was too much for Jacob to bear. Jacob's highly charged emotional response makes clear that he still blamed the brothers for Joseph's death, which was the reason he was so upset that they wanted to take the second child of Rachel with them on a perilous return journey to Egypt. One of the clear faults of Jacob is his unashamed and obtuse favoritism of Rachel's children. Yet these scandalously faulty character traits are an important part of the story.

None of the wrong sentiments of Jacob excuse the murderous passion towards Joseph by his brothers. In fact, later on we will see Judah accepting his father "as he is" and not "as he should be." This favoritism of Jacob is clearly wrongdoing, but one that will be graciously understood by Judah as he recalls his own wrongdoing towards Tamar due to his own favoritism toward his youngest son from a wife who had also died. (The story of Tamar claiming Judah's seed for her own by pretending to be a prostitute and Judah's failure to treat her justly suddenly becomes important, which finally explains why this seemingly unrelated story was inserted into the Joseph-related narrative. It had everything to do with it).

We read in Genesis 42:36:

וַיֹּאמֶר אֲלֵהֶם יַעֲקֹב אֲבִיהֶם אֹתִי שִׁכַּלְתֶּם יוֹסֵף אֵינֶנּוּ וְשִׁמְעוֹן אֵינֶנּוּ וְאֶת־בִּנְיָמִן תִּקָּחוּ עָלַי הָיוּ כֻלָּנָה:

*Their father Jacob said to them, "It is always me that you bereave: Joseph is no more and Simeon is no more, and now you would take away Benjamin. These things always happen to me!" (Gen. 42:36).*

Reuben tells his father that he can kill both of his sons if Benjamin does not return – a morally questionable and economically unsound business deal that once again shows Reuben as someone lacking

---

53    *Ibid.*

wisdom to lead, in spite of him being the eldest of the brothers and having some sense of conscience. Jacob rejects the request to allow Benjamin to go with the brothers to Egypt, preferring the comfort of knowing that Benjamin is safe, even though Simeon remains in an Egyptian jail (Gen. 42:36-38).

In this story salvation for Benjamin – and also for entire family of Israel – will come from Judah. He will turn the situation around by his self-sacrifice on behalf of Benjamin and, without realizing it, will forever establish his own tribe as a royal leader of the future nation of Israel. A possible reason Simeon was chosen to remain incarcerated in Egypt is because as Leah's second son (Gen.29:31-33), he could be an appropriate hostage for Benjamin, Rachel's second son. Simeon's name שִׁמְעוֹן (Shimon) is connected with the verb שָׁמַע (shamah), which means "to hear." In the context of the narrative, this meaning probably brings a hint of the brothers not paying heed to the cries of Joseph from the pit before he was auctioned off to Egypt. (Gen. 42:21-22). We read in Genesis 42:38:

וַיֹּאמֶר לֹא־יֵרֵד בְּנִי עִמָּכֶם כִּי־אָחִיו מֵת וְהוּא לְבַדּוֹ נִשְׁאָר וּקְרָאָהוּ אָסוֹן בַּדֶּרֶךְ אֲשֶׁר תֵּלְכוּ־בָהּ וְהוֹרַדְתֶּם אֶת־שֵׂיבָתִי בְּיָגוֹן שְׁאוֹלָה׃

*"My son must not go down with you, for his brother is dead and he alone is left. (Gen. 42:38).*

It is interesting that in this verse Jacob spoke of the second son of Rachel – Benjamin – as "my son," while failing to make any additional mention as to the second son of Leah – Simeon, who now was kept in captivity in Egypt (and who was mentioned in vs. 36). By stating that "only" Benjamin was left, he presumably meant of the sons of Rachel. Jacob betrays once again his parental shortcoming that first nurtured in the hearts of the brothers the sense of inferiority in his, their father's, house in comparison to the beloved and honored first son of Rachel. This theme is emphasized in the narrative over and over again. This is so because the brothers will, in the end, be tested as to whether or not they can now live with this unjustified favoritism of Jacob towards Rachel's children. Joseph will make sure that this is tested before reveals himself to them.

Jacob refuses to speak to his sons again about this matter. It is only after some time, when the supply of food brought from Egypt was almost gone, that the father again told the sons to go back to Egypt (not to save Simeon, but) to bring more food. It is also possible of course that Jacob here does not display any lack of care for the misfortune of Simeon, but instead is simply overwhelmed with fear and grief, thinking that Simeon, just as Joseph, is now as good as dead (the earlier mention in Gen. 42:36 may support this supposition). However, given everything we are told about Jacob's preferential treatment and his unfairness with love distribution in his family, it is likely that Jacob viewed the loss of Simeon as truly unfortunate "collateral damage," but what he really fears more than that is the loss of the last child of Rachel.

**Judah Steps Up**

What follows is the intense interaction between Jacob and one of his sons – Judah, who will eventually be trusted by Jacob with the leadership of his family and, thereby, the future nation of Israel.

In Genesis 43:8-9 we read:

וַיֹּאמֶר יְהוּדָה אֶל־יִשְׂרָאֵל אָבִיו שִׁלְחָה הַנַּעַר אִתִּי וְנָקוּמָה וְנֵלֵכָה וְנִחְיֶה וְלֹא נָמוּת גַּם־אֲנַחְנוּ גַם־אַתָּה גַּם־טַפֵּנוּ:

*Then Judah said to his father Israel, "Send the boy in my care, and let us be on our way, that we may live and not die – you and we and our children. (Gen. 43:8).*

אָנֹכִי אֶעֶרְבֶנּוּ מִיָּדִי תְּבַקְשֶׁנּוּ אִם־לֹא הֲבִיאֹתִיו אֵלֶיךָ וְהִצַּגְתִּיו לְפָנֶיךָ וְחָטָאתִי לְךָ כָּל־הַיָּמִים:

*I myself will be surety for him; you may hold me responsible: if I do not bring him back to you and set him before you, I shall stand guilty before you forever. (Gen. 43:9).*

כִּי לוּלֵא הִתְמַהְמָהְנוּ כִּי־עַתָּה שַׁבְנוּ זֶה פַעֲמָיִם:

*For we could have been there and back twice if we had not delayed." (Gen. 43:10).*

When Jacob tells his sons to get more food from Egypt, Judah – on behalf of all the brothers – refuses, citing the Egyptian vizier's condition to return only with their youngest brother accompanying them. Jacob then accuses Judah and the brothers of making a mistake by volunteering information about Benjamin. Judah defended their actions, stating that the vizier asked pointed and precise questions about their father and any more children, so they had no choice but to tell him the truth.

## Jacob as a Son of Abraham

Jacob reluctantly agrees. He instructs the sons to take gifts for the vizier, return the money the sons found in the bags and to also pay the expected price for grain. He then extends his blessing upon the children, trusting that *El Shaddai* will have mercy towards them and that both brothers will be released. This shows that, in the end, Jacob is a son of Abraham.

In this moment of great personal challenge (the feared loss of yet another beloved son) he was willing to trust *El Shaddai* with his most treasured Benjamin. Jacob is willing to stake everything on the God he has gotten to know through his rocky but redemptive sojourns. "The father invokes this old name for God and hopes for mercy. Everything is staked on that one name. Injured Jacob believes more than his sons. He dares to think of a new possibility. In his boldness, he breaks the cycle of his own grief and loss. And at the same time, he breaks the sons' spiral of betrayal and deception. Jacob is a picture of faithfulness that permits newness. He is able to care and grieve and therefore to hope."[54]

## Joseph Meets Benjamin

When the brothers arrived in Egypt, Joseph, upon the sight of Benjamin (probably from behind the scenes), instructed his steward to welcome the men into his own house and to prepare a festive meal. The first thing that the brothers hurried to tell Joseph's steward was that somehow the last time when they were in Egypt their money was returned to them, so they had brought that silver back. The silver will continue to follow them throughout the story, echoing the silver they received as a payment for their brother Joseph when he was sold into slavery. We read in Genesis 43:23 a telling explanation (even if contrived):

שָׁלוֹם לָכֶם אַל־תִּירָאוּ אֱלֹהֵיכֶם וֵאלֹהֵי אֲבִיכֶם נָתַן לָכֶם מַטְמוֹן בְּאַמְתְּחֹתֵיכֶם
כַּסְפְּכֶם בָּא אֵלָי וַיּוֹצֵא אֲלֵהֶם אֶת־שִׁמְעוֹן:

*"All is well with you; do not be afraid. Your God, the God of your father, must have put treasure in your bags for you. I got your payment." And he brought out Simeon to them. (Gen. 43:23).*

The steward welcomed them in, washed their feet and took care of their donkeys as well. The brothers laid out all the gifts they brought for the vizier, expecting him to arrive at some point later, since they understood from the steward that the vizier was planning to dine with them. When Joseph arrived, the brothers again bowed themselves to the ground before him. Just like Jacob before Esau when he returned the stolen blessing of the first-born and made a rightful restitution payment to Esau, the brothers, too, continue to bow down before Joseph, not once as the dream described, but many times over.

---

[54]  *Ibid.*, 339.

The first thing the vizier said to them upon his arrival was in the form of a question. We read about it in Genesis 43:27-28:

וַיִּשְׁאַל לָהֶם לְשָׁלוֹם וַיֹּאמֶר הֲשָׁלוֹם אֲבִיכֶם הַזָּקֵן אֲשֶׁר אֲמַרְתֶּם הַעוֹדֶנּוּ חָי׃

*He greeted them, and he said, "How is your aged father of whom you spoke? Is he still in good health?" (Gen. 43:27).*

וַיֹּאמְרוּ שָׁלוֹם לְעַבְדְּךָ לְאָבִינוּ עוֹדֶנּוּ חָי וַיִּקְּדוּ וַיִּשְׁתַּחֲוּ׃

*They replied, "It is well with your servant our father; he is still in good health." And they bowed and made obeisance. (Gen.43:28).*

As we will learn at the moment of Joseph's revelation of himself to the brothers, the issue of his father still being alive (something of which Joseph is not sure) is of utmost importance to him. It was not only that Joseph was violently taken from Jacob, but it was also Jacob who was violently taken from Joseph. What follows is an amazing display of Joseph's emotions as he first confirms with the brothers that the young boy standing with them is really Benjamin. He then proceeds, to the surprise of the brothers, to address the child in the kindest words possible.

We read in Genesis 43:29b אֱלֹהִים יָחְנְךָ בְּנִי *(Elohim yachnekha beni),* which literally means, "God be gracious to you, my son." One can almost feel the choking in Joseph's throat when he pronounced the appropriate words "my son," while in all reality he was desperately wanting to call him "my (full) brother." The time for that, however, has not yet come. The narrator then explains that once Joseph greeted Benjamin, he was overcome with emotion to such a degree that he was about to cry but, holding back his tears, he went to a different room and wept there. When he regained control of himself he ordered his servants to serve the meal.

## Joseph Tests His Brothers

He directed the steward to seat everyone in accordance to their age. The brothers were astonished at this, but complied. Their astonishment likely had to do with the steward's knowledge of the order of births. To their further amazement, the youngest brother Benjamin received a portion that far exceeded the portions of food received by all the others, irrespective of their seniority. We read in Genesis 43:34:

וַיִּשָּׂא מַשְׂאֹת מֵאֵת פָּנָיו אֲלֵהֶם וַתֵּרֶב מַשְׂאַת בִּנְיָמִן מִמַּשְׂאֹת כֻּלָּם חָמֵשׁ יָדוֹת וַיִּשְׁתּוּ וַיִּשְׁכְּרוּ עִמּוֹ:

*Portions were served them from his table; but Benjamin's portion was five times larger than that of anyone else. And they drank their fill with him. (Gen. 43:34).*

It appears that Joseph leveled against his brothers a series of tests. First, will they come back for one of their own (Simeon)? Second, will they display an envy-based reaction to Benjamin getting five times more food? The next and the ultimate test was to follow. Will the brothers defend at all cost the life the second son of Rachel (Benjamin)?

## Joseph's Ultimate Test for His Brothers

Joseph instructed his stewards to give as much grain to the brothers as they could carry, give back all the money they had brought, and to place Joseph's silver cup into the sack of Benjamin as they departed, seemingly with the vizier's mighty blessing and favor. As soon as they left the city, Joseph told the steward to stop the brothers and to accuse them of stealing his property. We read in Genesis 44:4b, 5b Joseph's precise instructions. The steward with accompanying guards were instructed to say to the brothers:

לָמָּה שִׁלַּמְתֶּם רָעָה תַּחַת טוֹבָה:

*Why did you repay good with evil? (Gen. 44:4b).*

100

הֲלוֹא זֶה אֲשֶׁר יִשְׁתֶּה אֲדֹנִי בּוֹ וְהוּא נַחֵשׁ יְנַחֵשׁ בּוֹ הֲרֵעֹתֶם אֲשֶׁר עֲשִׂיתֶם:

*It is the very one from which my master drinks and which he uses for divination. It was a wicked thing for you to do! (Gen. 44:5b).*

It is likely that the brothers knew exactly what cup the steward thought they had stolen as Joseph most likely used, or at least on purpose paraded it before them, perhaps even explaining his great abilities and connection with the divine. After all, Joseph's staff seemed to know things they simply could not have known naturally. Alter writes:

> The probable mechanism of divination in a goblet would be to interpret patterns on the surface of the liquid it contained or in drops running down its sides. Divination would have been a plausible activity on the part of a member of the high Egyptian bureaucracy, with its technology of soothsaying, but the emphasis it is given here is also linked with Joseph's demonstrated ability to predict the future and his superiority of knowledge in relation to his brothers.[55]

The brothers, unsuspecting of any set-up, defend themselves and foolishly proclaim that whoever is found with the cup in their sack should be put to death and the rest stay in Egyptian captivity indefinitely (Gen. 44:6-8). Though the proposed punishment sounded extreme, it is very much possible that the theft of a sacred item (like this divination cap) was traditionally understood in the Ancient Near East to deserve capital punishment. Interestingly enough, the brothers' words sound very similar to the exchange between Laban and Jacob (Gen. 31:32), and this is one of the ways we can see that these seemingly unconnected stories are actually connected. Laban does not find what he is looking for, but it is presumed that the price of the theft of Laban's gods is exacted in the

---

55  Alter, *Genesis: Translation and Commentary*, 260.

early death of Rachel later in the story when she gave birth to Benjamin.

Here, however, the divination cup is found, though it was not stolen by the brothers. They will, of course, be forgiven in the end, but only after they understand that this was somehow related to the great sin they had committed together 20 years prior against Joseph. When the brothers claimed that whoever stole the cup should die and the rest become slaves, the steward replied that though the proposed punishment fit the crime, a far more merciful option would be executed – only the guilty one will be held as a slave, the rest will go free. We read in Genesis 44:17:

חָלִילָה לִּי מֵעֲשׂוֹת זֹאת הָאִישׁ אֲשֶׁר נִמְצָא הַגָּבִיעַ בְּיָדוֹ הוּא יִהְיֶה־לִּי עָבֶד וְאַתֶּם עֲלוּ לְשָׁלוֹם אֶל־אֲבִיכֶם:

*"Far be it from me to act thus! Only he in whose possession the goblet was found shall be my slave: the rest of you go back in peace to your father." (Gen. 44:17).*

The language and role-playing are striking. Long ago, the brothers were probably upset not so much by Joseph but by Jacob, because of his preferential treatment of Joseph as Rachel's son. They turned their anger, however, not against their father, choosing to deal directly not with him but, predictably, with the object of Jacob's intense love – Joseph. In this brilliant scene, the steward echoes the words of Joseph's instructions to him and utters the words, "Far be it from me to act like that!" We have got to see the irony here. An Egyptian worshiper of pagan divinities has a sense of justice, while the children of Jacob, the members of the Covenant with Israel's God, do not. They were not in any way prepared for this turn of events and that was exactly Joseph's plan.

**Benjamin is Arrested**

All the brothers were searched and the last bag to be checked was that belonging to Benjamin, Rachel's second son and Joseph's full brother. Seeing that the cup was in fact found in Benjamin's sack, the brothers tore their clothes as a sign of grief and mounted their donkeys to return to the city with the steward. "Joseph's scheme, after all, is to make the brothers feel they are trapped in a network of uncanny circumstances they can neither control nor explain."[56] As all who want revenge, Joseph too wanted them, at least for a short time, to feel exactly what he had felt when he was thrown into the pit and sold to Egypt – perplexed, lost and alone. Thankfully by now revenge was not the center of Joseph's plan; rather, testing of the brothers was. Did the brothers remain the same? Did they change? Will they allow for the other son of Rachel, Benjamin, to be given over to slavery and possible death too? Will they abandon him as they had Joseph?

## Judah Acts Sacrificially

Judah, the one who originally conceived the plan to sell Joseph to Egypt, spoke up on behalf of the brothers, addressing the grand vizier. As Judah retells the entire drama (Gen. 44:18-30) he, without realizing it, speaks to his brother who is presumed dead (the fate of most slaves in Egypt after 20 years of intense labor). He tells him that "the father of Benjamin does not see meaning in life without his youngest son." The very issue that caused the negative feelings towards Joseph in the past is now accepted by a much older and more mature Judah. Judah still disagrees with Jacob, his father, but he now clearly understands him. He cannot bear seeing his father go through the pain of losing another son of Rachel and dying a depressed man who felt that he had completely failed in life. There is nothing that Judah fears more than his father's eternal disappointment and disapproval. Judah begs the vizier to allow him to exchange places with Benjamin. It is he who will remain a slave in Egypt and it is Benjamin that is to return to his father, Jacob (Gen. 44:30-34). Judah's tone of voice betrayed full determination. He was

---

[56]   *Ibid.*, 259.

ready and willing to save Benjamin even at the cost of his own freedom (or even life).

## Joseph Reveals Himself

Now is the moment that Joseph was waiting and hoping for with all of his heart. He wanted to reconcile with his brothers, but he wisely did not want to do that apart from seeing their truly repentant hearts. Joseph could hardly keep back his tears as he shouted for everyone to leave them alone in that room. Joseph's sobbing was so intense that the Egyptians heard it, and the news quickly was reported to the Pharaoh himself (Gen. 45:1-2). We read in Genesis 45:3 the words of Joseph's self-disclosure:

אֲנִי יוֹסֵף הַעוֹד אָבִי חָי וְלֹא־יָכְלוּ אֶחָיו לַעֲנוֹת אֹתוֹ כִּי נִבְהֲלוּ מִפָּנָיו:

*I am Joseph. Is my father still alive? But his brothers could not answer him, so dumfounded were they on account of him. (Gen. 45:3).*

The revelation אֲנִי יוֹסֵף *(ani Yosef)* "I am Joseph!" is quick and stunning. Joseph's very first question after this, הַעוֹד אָבִי חָי *(ha-od avi chai)* "Is my father still alive?" shows that, up until now, he had not really trusted anything that the brothers had said. That is, Joseph was not sure that the brothers had a living father. Now that he saw Judah's action in being willing to be left as a slave in Egypt forever, the hope of his father still being alive was suddenly resurrected in full force. Hence, his quick question to the brothers about his father.

What was revealed here was not for the eyes and ears of the Egyptian empire. The listening community of the children of Israel, however, were not asked by the narrator to leave the room together with the Egyptians (45:1), but were in fact invited to stay with the family. Think about it. The reader is permitted to witness a disclosure of the good news for Israel: The dead one is alive! The abandoned one has returned in power! The dream has had its way![57] Our God reigns.

## Joseph's Assurance

We read in Genesis 45:4b-8 Joseph's statement to his brothers:

אֲנִי יוֹסֵף אֲחִיכֶם אֲשֶׁר־מְכַרְתֶּם אֹתִי מִצְרָיְמָה:

*"I am your brother Joseph, he whom you sold into Egypt. (Gen. 45:4b).*

וְעַתָּה אַל־תֵּעָצְבוּ וְאַל־יִחַר בְּעֵינֵיכֶם כִּי־מְכַרְתֶּם אֹתִי הֵנָּה כִּי לְמִחְיָה שְׁלָחַנִי אֱלֹהִים לִפְנֵיכֶם:

*Now, do not be distressed or reproach yourselves because you sold me hither; it was to save life that God sent me ahead of you. (Gen. 45:5).*

וַיִּשְׁלָחֵנִי אֱלֹהִים לִפְנֵיכֶם לָשׂוּם לָכֶם שְׁאֵרִית בָּאָרֶץ וּלְהַחֲיוֹת לָכֶם לִפְלֵיטָה גְּדֹלָה:

*God has sent me ahead of you to ensure your survival on earth, and to save your lives in an extraordinary deliverance. (Gen. 45:7).*

וְעַתָּה לֹא־אַתֶּם שְׁלַחְתֶּם אֹתִי הֵנָּה כִּי הָאֱלֹהִים

*So, it was not you who sent me here, but God. (Gen. 45:8).*

Joseph told the brothers to go back to Jacob as quickly as they were able to tell him about Joseph and to bring everyone back with them so that the prophecy once given to Joseph in a dream would be fulfilled. Joseph will provide bread and sustenance to his entire family during these difficult times of famine in the entire Middle East. Two years of famine were over, but five more were still to come. The brothers needed to hurry. The good news for the house of Israel need not be kept secret any more. It needed to be told now.

---

57    Brueggemann, *Genesis: Interpretation*, 343.

It is interesting that Joseph does not demand from his brothers that they confess to their father the whole truth, realizing that the truth would probably be too traumatic for him to hear. The Torah leaves this to the imagination of the listening community of the children of Israel. He only instructs them to tell him of the good things that now await the family of Israel in Egypt.

## The Graciousness of Pharaoh

Pharaoh was very pleased when the report came to him that Joseph's brothers had come. The phraseology used points us to the possibility that Joseph had shared with Pharaoh the bitter, intimate details of his life and suffering, and perhaps both of them knew or suspected that sooner or later the brothers of Joseph would have to come to Egypt for bread. Joseph was prepared and so was Pharaoh as he extended his personal guarantees of well-being and prosperity to Joseph's family as soon as they reach Egypt (Gen. 45:16-20).

In Brueggemann's words: "The revelation breaks as news upon the entire family. The news is abrupt in a narrative that has been shaped in a quite secular way. This speech completely redefines the situation for all parties. Now the guilty fear of the brothers is superseded. The grief of the father is resolved. He had grieved unnecessarily, for what seemed death was God's way to life. The revengeful cunning of the successful brother is superseded. He has no need to triumph over his family. The guilt of the brothers, the grief of the father, and the revenge of Joseph are all used as means for this disclosure of the hidden call of God. None of that matters now, for the whole family is now brought to a new moment."[58]

The story does read like a drama with a very moving conclusion. The Torah's portrayal of Jacob and his emotion at hearing, and at first disbelieving, that Joseph was still alive is highlighted. That which

---

[58] Brueggemann, *Genesis: Interpretation*, 345-6.

could have been stated in one summarized sentence (as was almost always the case in Genesis earlier) is opened up and savored by the storyteller (Gen. 45:25-28) to be truly felt by its original hearers – the Israelites who had left Egypt and were on the way to the Promised Land, meeting all the struggles of this perilous journey.

The story does not end here, but goes on. There is so much more that could be said about the Book of Genesis, but perhaps it should be left for another time. After all, this story was never meant to be read, considered and understood only once, but rather lived and relived from year to year by all children of the scandalous but truly remarkable man who struggled with God.

# BIBLIOGRAPHY

Alter, Robert. 1998. *Genesis.* New York: W.W. Norton.

Berlin, Adele, and Marc Zvi Brettler. 2014. *The Jewish Study Bible: Torah, Nevi'im, Kethuvim,* 2nd edition. New York: Oxford University Press.

Brueggemann, Walter. 2010. *Genesis.* Louisville: Westminster John Knox Press.

Levenson, Ron D. "Genesis Introductions and Annotations." In *The Jewish Study Bible. Tanakh Translation,* edited by Adele Berlin and Marc Zvi Brettler, New York: Oxford University Press, 2014.

Sacks, Jonathan. 2009. *Covenant & Conversation: a Weekly Reading of the Jewish Bible.* Genesis: The Book of Beginnings. New Milford, CT: Maggid Books & The Orthodox Union.

Sacks, Jonathan. 2015. *Not In God's Name.* New York: Schocken Books.

Made in the USA
Middletown, DE
24 August 2019